JOY

IN THE

WAR

DANIEL & AMBER PIERCE

CHARISMA HOUSE

MOST CHARISMA HOUSE BOOK GROUP products are available at special quantity discounts for bulk purchase for sales promotions, premiums, fund-raising, and educational needs. For details, call us at (407) 333-0600 or visit our website at www.charismahouse.com.

JOY IN THE WAR by Daniel and Amber Pierce
Published by Charisma House
Charisma Media/Charisma House Book Group
600 Rinehart Road, Lake Mary, Florida 32746

JOY

IN THE

WAR

burden of spiritual battles and will show you how to seek restoration from trauma and become whole in the calling that God has for you.

—AVI MIZRACHI
FOUNDING PASTOR, ADONAI ROI
(THE LORD IS MY SHEPHERD) CONGREGATION;
FOUNDER, DUGIT OUTREACH CENTER, TEL AVIV, ISRAEL

This observation sets the tone for Daniel and Amber Pierce's triumphant journey that has been beautifully chronicled in their new rendering, *Joy in the War: Expand Your Ability to Embrace Hope in the Heat of Battle*: "There is a peace that comes with the knowledge that God is in control of our times and seasons. Acts 17:26 affirms this. 'From one man he made all the nations, that they should inhabit the whole earth; and he marked out their appointed times in history and the boundaries of their lands.'" The Pierces' exploits have traversed lands, but their submitted hearts have opened every door as God has led the charge for them to passionately pursue and overtake every enemy to attain joy for the victory as each challenge is conquered. With Israel front and center as passionate inspiration, this book infuses with joy as each battle unfolds and victory is declared.

—KENT MATTOX
SENIOR PASTOR, WORD ALIVE
INTERNATIONAL OUTREACH

Into a world being shaken by the clash of two kingdoms, God is releasing a clear sound through Daniel and Amber's book *Joy in the War*. Jesus told us that in this world we would have tribulation, war, but to be of good cheer; He had overcome it all. Knowing that Christ is the center from where life flows is the anchor point for everyone who is committed to following the plans God has for their life. The truths contained in this book will serve as a guide to all who seek to follow after Him and for those trying to understand "Why Israel?" I was captured from the first chapter and would recommend this to all who are on a personal journey to fulfill the call of God on their lives.

—JANE HANSEN HOYT
PRESIDENT AND CEO, AGLOW INTERNATIONAL

We have had the honor of being fellow laymen in the work of the kingdom with the Pierce family for years. They have a legacy of love for the body of Christ and the people of Israel, and Daniel and Amber have carried that passion and dedication into their life and ministry. In their timely new book they take on the current battle that is breaking down the hope of so many, and they bring insight and biblical truth that will help restore peace and joy even in life's toughest seasons.

—MARCUS AND JONI LAMB
FOUNDERS, DAYSTAR TELEVISION NETWORK

If we ever needed this book, *Joy in the War*, it is today. Daniel and Amber Pierce share insight on how to overcome and revive joy with transparency and wisdom beyond their years. My heart was uplifted as I read the pages of this book. Joy does, indeed, come in the morning.

—CINDY JACOBS
GENERALS INTERNATIONAL
DALLAS, TEXAS

I have known Daniel and Amber since 2011, when they moved to Tel Aviv and began their journey in ministry there. Over the last ten years, we have become good friends, and I have been able to walk with them and watch as they have grown in their walk with the Lord and the maturity of their call in Israel. I was so excited when I found out that Daniel and Amber had completed this work, *Joy in the War*. This book reflects many of the struggles and challenges that Israelis face on a day-to-day basis. I believe this book will instill joy and encourage you to seek strength in the Lord. *Joy in the War* will minister to many who have experienced the loss and

Visit the author's website at gloryofzionjerusalem.org.

Library of Congress Cataloging-in-Publication Data: An application to register this book for cataloging has been submitted to the Library of Congress.
International Standard Book Number: 978-1-62999-982-1
E-book ISBN: 978-1-62999-983-8

21 22 23 24 25 — 9 8 7 6 5 4 3 2 1
Printed in the United States of America

We would like to dedicate Joy in the War to our children,
Lily, Elijah, and Charles Pierce. They have endured the challenges
of life and childhood in a foreign country so that our family
could continue to serve the Lord in every capacity that God has
called us to. In that we have all been tremendously blessed.

I pray that the next generation will learn to walk in the joy
of the Lord, as He has shown us His joy even in the hardest
of times. We would like to thank Daniel's father, Chuck Pierce,
and mother, Pam Pierce, for their love, support, and guidance, as
they have never failed to encourage us in our marriage and walk
with the Lord. We would also like to honor Amber's father,
Jed Sauce, and mother, Barbra Sauce,
in loving memory.

Contents

Acknowledgments

W E WOULD LIKE to thank Chuck Pierce for mentoring us in our spiritual walk and contending for a place of maturity in our faith and the faith of this generation. Throughout the process of our writing *Joy in the War*, Chuck never stopped encouraging us to minister out of our testimony and allow the Lord to build our faith in a way that would produce strength for our future and the future of those God has placed in our lives.

We would like to thank Pam Pierce for being the mother that God has called her to be. Pam was an English major, and without her tireless work I would not have developed the skills necessary to write *Joy in the War*. Thank you, Mom, for teaching me from a young age to seek the Lord always and place my faith at the center of my life.

Special thanks go to Brian Kooiman for all the hard work he has done to make *Joy in the War* possible. He spent many hours editing and communicating with Charisma House editors on our behalf. We also want to thank you, Brian, for all your encouragement over the years and administrative efforts that have allowed us to continue our ministry at home and abroad.

Special thanks also go to Avi and Chaya Mizrachi, who welcomed us to be part of their congregation in Tel Aviv and helped us establish our lives in Israel. They have been good friends and an ongoing source of encouragement and mentorship that we desperately needed living in a foreign land. Thank you, Avi and Chaya, for your guidance and willingness to help us in understanding your culture and becoming a part of Israel.

I must also thank all the spiritual leaders and authorities that God has placed in our lives for the purpose of pushing us forward in our walk with Him and who took the time to raise us up in our call. God has placed many people in our lives who have acted as mothers and fathers, continually encouraging us to seek the Lord without ceasing.

Foreword

FULFILL YOUR DESTINY— ENJOY **LIFE**!

J OY IN THE WAR is an amazing book. Everyone should read it. Of course I'm a little biased because the authors, Daniel and Amber, are my son and daughter-in-law. Over the years, however, I've watched them go through many trials and tests that have resulted in the powerful testimony reflected in the following pages. As you read, you will be empowered to overcome your own trials and tests. You will also gain a better understanding of our alignment and calling to Israel as believers.

From the beginning, when God saw the earth in confusion and chaos, He planned for a people who would move from chaos into multiplication. He spoke! Chaos subsided, and abundance began. This is the essence of spiritual life. Moving from desolation into a new level of abundance is always the Lord's purpose. When Yeshua, Jesus of Nazareth, defined why He came or was sent to the earth, He said, "The thief comes only in order to steal and kill and destroy. I came that they may have and enjoy life, and have it in abundance [to the full, till it overflows]" (John 10:10, AMP). Many Christians, and even those seeking to understand their earthly purpose, never realize that the One who was sent to redeem them purposed them to "enjoy life." Before this portion of the verse we find Jesus declaring, "I am the Door; anyone who enters through Me will be saved [and will live forever], and will go in and out [freely], and find pasture (spiritual security)" (v. 9, emphasis added). This is meant to help you enter the Door (called Christ) into a new dimension of abundance.

About seventy-five people work for our ministry. I remember four years ago being in a quandary because I wanted to give Christmas bonuses to those workers who had served faithfully, yet the finances didn't seem to be there. I knew the holidays could be a tremendous blessing and incredibly stressful at the same time. While pondering what to do, the Lord whispered John 10:10 into my ear. It is a key verse that has directed my life. However, this time, His voice illuminated deep within my spirit the portion of the scripture that says, "I came that they might have and *enjoy life.*"

Then the Spirit of God prompted to me, "Enjoy those who have served and bless them." Faith comes from hearing when the Spirit speaks to us, and God wanted me to move by faith. A word of warning here, though. When taking a step of faith like this, we must be sure we have heard the voice of God correctly and not move in presumption. I discerned this was the Spirit of God speaking, and the instruction was clear. I was to take what we *did not* have and bless each one who had served. As I obeyed that divine order, a supernatural joy began to overwhelm me. That joy was indeed a miracle because it did not come from me, yet God had another surprise in store. The next morning, when all I had given (which was a substantial amount) was already on the way through the mail, I noticed another miracle had occurred. Anxiety I had carried for years as the result of a deep trauma (you will read about this in the afterword) had lifted. That old, bad friend was gone, and the joy of the Lord replaced that portion within my soul and spirit. That is what this book is about.

Each chapter that Daniel and Amber write will bring you into a more liberated experience of joy and freedom. Warfare is conflict, and amid the conflict we can lose our joy. Joy produces strength. When we don't sense the life of Christ flowing through us, we need to ask the Lord, "What has happened to my passion? Amid my circumstance, Lord, did I get tired and quit withstanding?" In truth, we can pray until we turn blue. We can do all sorts of religious activities. But if we don't resist the enemy during that trial (the temptation toward passivity and all other temptations), and if we don't let that trial bring the working of the cross into us, then we won't enter the passion and fullness of life that the Lord has for each of us. Having God's passion as we walk in wisdom and revelation is the key to protecting ourselves from becoming outwitted by the enemy.

Yeshua Himself prophesied that a triumphant people filled with the Father's revelation would arise and prevail against hell's gates. This refers to a people who will do exploits! They are an apostolic people who take God's resources and let Him multiply them for His glory. They are a modern people, yet they resemble those ancients who crossed over the Jordan River 476 years after God spoke them into existence when He communicated to their father, Abraham. They are a people who will build a new prototype for today and unlock a kingdom mentality that hell cannot withstand. They will have centers for gatherings that are filled with the fire of His glory! Some of the real trials have come in establishing a Glory Center in the middle of Jerusalem. Daniel and Amber are the overseers of the Justice Center—Glory of Zion International Ministries in Jerusalem.

In Matthew 16 the Father revealed to Peter who Yeshua was, and a prophecy came forth. Unlocked revelation releases prophecy! Jesus released a prophecy for ages to come.

> Then Jesus answered him, "Blessed [happy, spiritually secure, favored by God] are you, Simon son of Jonah, because flesh and blood (mortal man) did not reveal this to you, but My Father who is in heaven. And I say to you that you are Peter, and on this rock I will build My church; and the gates of Hades (death) will not overpower it [by preventing the resurrection of the Christ]. I will give you the keys (authority) of the kingdom of heaven; and whatever you bind [forbid, declare to be improper and unlawful] on earth will have

[already] been bound in heaven, and whatever you loose [permit, declare lawful] on earth will have [already] been loosed in heaven."

—Matthew 16:17–19, amp

I am honored to be numbered along with these people of triumph. I came to know the Father of my spirit when I was a young man. He opened the heavenly vault and gave me a glimpse of His blessings. He showed me the war and the army of darkness determined to keep us from accessing these blessings. He taught my hands to war and my heart to worship. His voice has become my life. Daily He is still teaching me to experience why I am here: *to enjoy life!*

I have come to know the One who paid the price for my freedom. The Father sacrificed the Son to unlock all spiritual blessings in heavenly places. These blessings have amassed through the years of your bloodline dwelling in the earth. Some of your predecessors may have added to these blessings through their obedience. Some may have accessed the blessings that the Father created for them and manifested these blessings on earth. Others may have rejected these blessings and deferred them to your time to be accessed. Whatever the case, He came that you may *enjoy* the *abundance* of His blessings! I hope reading Daniel's and Amber's words accomplishes its purpose: to produce wisdom that helps you outwit the enemy. Most of all, I pray that this book helps you to fulfill your destiny—*to enjoy life!*

—Dr. Chuck D. Pierce
President, Glory of Zion International Ministries
President, Global Spheres

PART I:

MAKING SENSE

OF THE

PAST

Chapter 1

SUBMITTING TO THE **JOURNEY**

T HE MOMENT WE make a personal decision to follow Jesus as Lord and Savior, a new journey in our life begins. More than a mere choice to walk with the Lord, it is a decision to enter into a covenant relationship with Him. This relationship impacts the course of our future. If we learn to view life as a journey with God and submit to the path He unfolds before us, our faith will be renewed time and again.

God has a way of bringing most believers to a point in their lives when they realize they are flawed and weak and their best efforts fall short. They come to a firm understanding that they can't do the Christian life in their own strength. This is a good place to arrive, because it's when our weaknesses are submitted to Him that we become strong. God delights in taking our failures and limitations, our trials and tests, and turning them into our unique testimony. This testimony is our strength!

I have met many people who assumed that I (Daniel) have always walked with the Lord because I grew up in a Christian home. When I was young, my parents spent a lot of time taking us to church and reading the Bible in our home, but God still had to bring me to the point of a personal relationship with Him.

I was just five years old when my journey with the Lord began. With Christmas only two weeks away, I had been pondering all the toys on my list and growing increasingly anxious because

I knew my parents couldn't afford them. After checking the list thoroughly to ensure not a single toy was missed, a hollow, sinking feeling began to fill the pit of my stomach. In that moment, a light of understanding flashed inside my young mind of how easy it had been for greed and selfishness to consume me. Time seemed to slow to a crawl as I grew more uncomfortable with each passing second. Nothing could make that gnawing feeling in my gut go away. Suddenly those toys on my list began to lose their luster. It didn't matter what I got for Christmas. None of those gifts would make me happy. This was quite a serious revelation for a five-year-old.

By Sunday morning I had reached a point of not being able to stand this feeling anymore, and that's when God began speaking to me. Suddenly a supernatural peace that I'd never experienced before enveloped me. Along with the peace came a knowing that Jesus was the answer I had been looking for. Unsure of what to do next, I approached my mother, who was sitting in front of the bathroom mirror, preparing for church. Standing there crying, I told her about my experience and how I wanted to accept Jesus into my life. That morning, I decided to follow the Lord. I still remember the feeling of grace and freedom that washed over me as my mother took me by the hands and prayed. God reminds me often of that first step in my relationship with Him. Even though it was a simple act, I was never the same after that moment. And that's the way God works. Because we are all like children, His ways are uncomplicated.

Most of us go through life pursuing what we think will make us happy only to discover it's a dead-end road. Yet it is there, at the end, we face a choice. Do we follow Jesus or the ways of this world? One writer put it this way: "When we reach the end, God's best begins...but only if we let it."[1]

I remember having several other powerful experiences with the Lord as a child. When I was eight years old, my dad took me to a missionary convention where booths were set up from different nations. Each booth had a representative handing out information on what God was doing in that particular country. At the convention the Holy Spirit began drawing me to the Middle Eastern nations, and a strong conviction filled me that international ministry would somehow be in my future. At the time, I had no way of knowing that the winding journey God had for my life would eventually take me, along with my wife and children, to Israel.

> Enter through the narrow gate. For wide is the gate and broad is the road that leads to destruction, and many enter through it. But small is the gate and narrow the road that leads to life, and only a few find it.
>
> —MATTHEW 7:13–14

I wish I could tell you that I faithfully lived for the Lord every day since my salvation story began at age five, but I'd be lying. When I turned sixteen, the ways of the world allured me, and I decided to live for myself for a while. That decision marked the beginning of a dark era in my life that lasted six years, until I was twenty-two. During that time, it became abundantly clear that it was impossible to live a life in the gray area between a relationship with Jesus and our sinful natures. Trying to live a lukewarm existence in the gray area leaves a person miserable. Fortunately, one year before I met my wife, Amber, the Lord began to draw me back into a deeper relationship with Him.

WORKING IN LAW ENFORCEMENT

At nineteen I went to work full-time for the Denton County Sheriff's Office as a correctional officer while attending the University of North Texas Police Academy at night. Needless to say, it was an extremely busy time.

Working in the jail was a transitional period in my life. The atmosphere of incarceration has a way of changing a person's perception. I can still hear those massive steel doors rolling shut and locking behind me at the beginning of every shift. Though I knew I would get out when my shift was over, it felt like I was the one being imprisoned as the outside world got cut off from me. Speaking to inmates often caused me to lose faith in humanity, as some of them seemed to have no moral compass. Some days you could almost cut the tension with a knife, and fights would break out over the simplest things, such as whose turn it was to watch TV or do the chores.

Working in the jail provides the perfect training ground for law enforcement officers who want to work patrol. Criminals don't stop being criminals just because they are locked up; they often lie, cheat, or steal to get what they want.

One night in class the police academy instructor made a comment that deeply impacted me. "Law enforcement is not a profession for those who don't know who they are," he said, "and we had better get grounded in something." Then he held up a Bible and told us, "You better get grounded in God or you will find yourself at the bottom of a bottle. Many officers over the years have become alcoholics and lost their marriages or worse."

After working in the jail for five years, a job opportunity with the Celina Police Department opened up for me. I was excited to finally go to work on patrol. Celina is a small town located on the border of Collin County and Denton County. The police chief at the time was a friend of mine, and I had worked with some of the other officers in the past, so this seemed a good place to start my law enforcement career. God blessed me tremendously for the first two years of my service there, and I would define that time in my life as an open heaven season—a time when God was speaking to me so routinely that it felt like an open conversation. Each day in the field, I could see how the Lord was preparing me for the future.

The city experienced a period of rapid growth and prosperity, almost doubling in size in only a few years. As my relationship with the Lord began to deepen, I would often seek Him while out patrolling the streets. I found that the more I prayed, the more God would show me things and position me in the right places at the right times. It was uncanny. At the beginning of my shifts

I would find a quiet place to park for a few minutes and pray for God's protection and that He would reveal any attack of the enemy against the city. Almost like clockwork God began to answer these prayers, and there were many occasions where I believe He supernaturally intervened in situations that changed the course of someone's life.

LEARNING TO HEAR GOD'S VOICE

I had been working for the police department several months when Amber and I made our first trip to Israel. My dad, Chuck Pierce, had invited us to go with him as he ministered there and spent time experiencing the land. As we walked in the footsteps of Jesus and other biblical characters, God's Word came alive! Our understanding of Scripture was illuminated, and we could feel the Lord drawing us.

The trip was incredible; however, only a few hours before we boarded our return flight to Texas, I developed a high fever. When we got home, I called my police chief and explained that I was sick and couldn't work. He told me we were short-staffed and I needed to come in anyway but could sit at the station unless dispatched to a call. For three days I sat there with cold chills, hardly able to move. On the fourth night I started feeling a bit better, when suddenly God quickened in my spirit that I needed to get up and patrol the city.

It was 11 p.m. when I left the station and dragged myself to the patrol car. At 11:30 I pulled into Carter Ranch, a large subdivision on the outskirts of the city that was under construction at the time. Unfinished buildings are an invitation for thieves to steal copper piping and tools or equipment that may have been left on-site, which is why police routinely look for parked cars near construction sites. Upon entering the subdivision, I noticed a small gray car with its lights off parked in the dark. The driver was standing outside his vehicle, and when he saw my patrol car, he jumped in his car and sped down one of the back roads.

Quickly tailing him, I passed where the car had been parked

and noticed a woman's purse lying in the middle of the road. My heart pounded as I raced to catch up with the suspicious driver, who had now turned onto the main highway. I could still see the little gray car in the distance, so I punched the gas pedal to catch up. After hitting the overhead lights, I flipped on the siren and called for backup, not knowing whether the suspect would stop or continue to run. Much to my relief, he pulled over. Still, the situation could be good or bad; a police officer never knows. For any of you who might have seen a high-speed pursuit on *Cops* or the news, they tend to be quite dangerous.

When I approached the vehicle, I found a thirty-five-year-old man behind the wheel and two underage girls sitting in the back seat. Both were teens and obviously intoxicated. None of them could answer my questions as to why they were parked in the back of a neighborhood.

When my backup arrived, I asked the driver to stand with the other officer outside the vehicle so I could speak to the girls privately. It turned out they had recently met the guy at a softball practice and left without their parents' knowledge to go drinking with him. When I ran the driver's information with Collin County dispatch, it came back that he was a known sex offender and currently on parole for sexual assault of a minor. Obviously the girls were not aware of the danger they were in that night. We found several partially consumed bottles of alcohol in the trunk and arrested the driver for providing alcohol to minors. Then I called the girls' parents to come pick them up.

Several months later I was contacted to testify in a parole hearing concerning this case. At the end of the day, the judge revoked the driver's parole and sent him back to prison for the incident at Carter Ranch. After the hearing, one of the girls and her mother approached me in the hall outside the courtroom. With tears in her eyes the mother told me that she knew God had sent me to protect her daughter that night. The Holy Spirit had prompted me to leave the station that night at that precise moment and patrol that neighborhood. He wants to guide you in your life situations as well.

AN APPOINTMENT WITH GOD

On another occasion, I was sitting in my patrol car eating breakfast when dispatch notified me that Denton County was chasing a pickup truck and would be coming through our city. I raced out to the northwest border of the city to meet the county units as the pursuit crossed the border into Collin County. Before I reached the county line, the pursuit turned east and then back to the north. Unable to catch up, I drove out to the highway that runs through the city from south to north in the hopes of locating the suspect vehicle and pursuing units. Several other agencies had joined in at that point, and there were at least six patrol cars behind the pickup truck. The whole time I was praying that God would place me in the right place at the right time if I was supposed to be involved in this situation.

From the highway I could see the action in the distance as the pursuit continued parallel to my position all the way into Grayson County. The sound of sirens from my own police car seemed to fade away as my speedometer pinned out at 130 mph. I remembered my police academy training about a phenomemon called "outrunning the sirens," but experiencing it firsthand was surreal. Dispatchers from both Collin County and Grayson County were helping me navigate as the chase was now well outside my jurisdiction.

About twenty minutes later the pickup truck ran out of gas, and the two suspects jumped out and sprinted through a cornfield. On the other side was a patch of woods they dove into. Not long afterwards I made it to the staging area where the other officers involved were preparing to enter the woods. One of the suspects had already been apprehended, but the driver was still at large and possibly armed. A sergeant on scene told me they could use all the help they could get, so I went to the patrol car and pulled out my AR-15 rifle and checked the ammo.

There were ten officers, including myself, lined up at the edge of the woods about a hundred yards apart waiting for the order to move. When the signal came, we walked silently through the woods, our heads swiveling, searching for any movement. With a pounding heart and sweaty palms I thought, "Where would I be if I was out here running from the police?"

I found a creek bottom and decided to follow it. Everywhere the creek turned, a brush pile had collected. As I stealthily approached one of these piles, I noticed slight movement as if something was inside. Peering closer yet maintaining my distance, I could just make out a man's tennis shoe hidden under the leaves and branches. Taking cover behind an oak tree, I pointed my rifle and began yelling for the suspect to surrender. Several other officers ran to assist. The suspect crawled out and was placed in handcuffs.

When I made it back to my patrol car, the time stamped on the computer that records the moment an officer checks out on scene read exactly 0902 AM. The road we caught the suspect on was FM 902 in Grayson County. I knew at that moment God had answered my prayer and placed me in the right place at the right time to bring justice into a situation. I have thought about this experience many times over the years as God continues to remind me how imperative it is that we are in the right place at the right time.

SUPERNATURAL PROTECTION

One morning, I was dispatched to a traffic accident where a small car had been hit by a pickup truck. While on the way to the accident I learned that the driver of the car was twenty-two years old and had four small children in the vehicle who had not been wearing seat belts. My heart almost stopped when I arrived on scene and saw the car upside down in a ditch. A witness immediately informed me that two of the children had been thrown from the car. After calling for medical helicopters to be placed on standby, I ran to check on the occupants. My mind braced itself for the possible scene that awaited, but when I reached the car, something unexpected made me breathe a sigh of relief. A metal grate covered the ditch, and the car had landed upside down right on top of the grate. The two children who were thrown from the car had fallen through the metal bars and into the bottom of the ditch. Both children were saved because the grate had stopped the car from crushing them.

A few minutes later four helicopters landed in a field across the street, and all the victims were evacuated to a trauma center in Dallas. Later that afternoon, I called the hospital and found that the four children and driver had sustained only minor injuries. It could only have been the hand of God that saved those kids. Everyone present knew they had witnessed a miracle.

During my time working in law enforcement, God used many such experiences to teach me. One thing I learned is that God decides our timing, even to the point of life and death. I have seen situations that should have killed someone but didn't, and others that took life without explanation. I came to the understanding that my life is in God's hands, and it gave me the faith and courage to walk into dangerous situations. There is a peace that comes with the knowledge that God is in control of our times and seasons. Acts 17:26 affirms this. "From one man he made all the nations, that they should inhabit the whole earth; and he marked out their appointed times in history and the boundaries of their lands."

A CALL TO MINISTRY

After those first two years with the police department, the city of Celina started making some changes that led to the hiring of a new city manager. A few months later the city manager decided to fire the heads of several city departments and replace them, including the chief of police. As it turned out, our new chief had been a captain in a much larger city before coming to Celina and had an entirely different ideology about law enforcement. Working for a smaller department allows the officers to

11

maintain a more personal relationship with the community. I enjoyed that aspect. Department policy in bigger cities tends to focus on liability concerns more than community values and winds up taking much of the decision-making ability away from the individual officer.

Many things small-town police officers do to administrate the well-being of the community could get them fired if they were working for a larger department. My reason for getting into law enforcement in the first place was to make a difference in the lives of those around me. When my ability to serve in that capacity was curtailed, I knew my time with the city was drawing to a close. I worked for the Celina Police Department two more years before making the decision to leave and seek the Lord for our next step.

Just a couple weeks after I left my job with the city, my dad once again invited us to join him in Israel. At the time, I didn't have a clear vision for the future and still felt a bit mixed up over the situation with the police department. The possibility of working for another agency or a security company had opened up for me, but for some reason I couldn't come to a place of peace over continuing down that path. I felt very conflicted. Law enforcement was all I knew. My stomach was in knots over the idea of learning an entirely new profession. Still, policework had been hard on the family at times, and Amber was in favor of a change of pace. We would soon see, however, that God had our times in His hands. The Holy Spirit was guiding our every step, even though outward circumstances seemed to scream the opposite. While we were in Israel, several things happened that would alter the course of our future. It was on that trip that the Lord began calling us into ministry and we saw Him open the door for us to move to Israel.

Next, Amber will share the experience from her perspective because she had a supernatural dream that God used to speak vision into our lives.

MOVING TO ISRAEL

When you are meant to live in Israel, you are like a piece in
a puzzle; the puzzle isn't complete without you, and you are
not complete without being in the puzzle.

—AMBER PIERCE

To give you a little history on me, I (Amber) grew up in an
unbelieving home where witchcraft was part of my mother's
belief system and abuse was a complex part of our family.
After abusing drugs and alcohol, I came to faith at the age of
twenty-three while attending Texas Woman's University. My
experience in the Holy Spirit was overwhelming, instantaneous,
and a complete transformation. God wasted no time using me.
I became president of Youth for Christ and a fervent evangelist,
leading many young women to Jesus. At Glory of Zion ministries
in Texas my calling was affirmed, and I began to grow in the
Holy Spirit.

I had met Daniel soon after my salvation. Eventually we were
married, and I supported him in all his work in the police force
and his ministry. Little did I know that a dream, a prophetic call,
and a word of dedication spoken over Daniel would bring about
a dramatic change to pursuing God's call on our lives together
in Israel.

On that second trip to Israel we stayed with some good
friends at their home in Jerusalem. One night I had a dream
that we moved to Israel. I saw myself walking down the stone
streets of the Old City with a strong impression that Israel was
my home. I just knew that I knew. When I woke up and told
Daniel about the dream, he looked baffled and exclaimed, "No
way!"

At the time, I dismissed the whole idea even though the
dream felt incredibly real, like a night vision. Later that day,
Daniel, his father, Chuck, and I went out to tour Jerusalem
and shop in the Old City. We walked up and down the stone
streets, fully absorbing the bustling market culture around

us. Hanging thick in the air were the aromas of exotic spices, incense, leather goods, and carpets. Shopkeepers stood outside the doors, hawking their wares, enticing the casbah of tourists and locals into their stores. The walled portion of the Old City is also the home of many religious pilgrims and their faithful hosts. Jewish-quarter residents always seem to be rushing somewhere, going about the business of their different sects and religious institutions.

The streets are also a kaleidoscope of sounds as families and different groups worship at the Western Wall (the Kotel). Hourly ringing of church bells mixes with the Muslim call to prayer that blares five times daily. The Orthodox Christians—Syrian Orthodox, Greek Orthodox, and Catholics—go to their churches. Each member of "the faithful" has his or her unique dress, identifying which one he or she belongs to. On almost every street corner you'll find tour guides giving lectures to groups from different nations in every imaginable language. Jerusalem provides a unique foreign tourism experience; it's certainly not the kind of place that feels like home, at least in the beginning.

When we returned to the home we were staying in, Chuck asked us to join him in a meeting with a group of spiritual leaders from Tel Aviv. Out of the blue, Chuck turned to one of the leaders and stated, "I think Daniel and Amber will be moving to Israel!"

In complete shock Daniel looked at me and asked, "Did you tell my dad about your dream?"

"No!" I ardently replied, shaking my head.

At that point, I told Chuck about my dream experience the night before. His words had been a confirmation. After this unexpected turn of events, Chuck calmly said he had always known that Daniel would be serving in Israel, and he had prophetically written in Daniel's baby book that Daniel would be given to Israel in a time of war. Chuck and his wife, Pam, had dedicated Daniel to that purpose after he was born. Wow. Now that it was out in the open, the dream was coming to pass before our eyes, and it was all happening very fast.

I have found that dreams are one of the ways God speaks to me and part of how He goes before us to prepare the way. His appointed dreams are sovereign; as we watch, rest, and come into agreement with Him, He opens the way for their fulfillment. This is part of submitting to the journey He has for us—not by overstriving but by trusting, learning, and being willing to take steps as His path unfolds before us.

Now that we knew Israel would be our new home, we needed to know what part of Israel we would reside in. Looking over a map of Israel, Daniel and I visualized living in Jerusalem, but we felt it wasn't time yet, so we decided to move to the coast. Chuck wrote a letter to a leader in Tel Aviv, who warmly invited us to come to his assembly. We moved there first and were unconditionally loved and embraced. Tel Aviv was where we would form the close relationships for the rest of our time in Israel and for the rest of our lives.

CLOSING OUR LIVES IN TEXAS

When we got back to Texas, Chuck asked Daniel, "When are you going to get a job again with a police force?"

"I thought we were moving to Israel," Daniel replied.

"One condition," Chuck said, "is that you can't go to Israel with any debt. We want to see it unfold under God's hand, and He will bring it to pass."

As it turned out, all the debt that Daniel had accrued in his young life without having a long work record was taken care of through his retirement account, which paid off the debts to the penny! After that, our home near Frisco sold quickly. We sold our cars. Things were moving along speedily as we prepared to leave. Sometimes it felt too speedily. Not all of it was easy. For me the hardest parts were giving up a home we loved, friends and family, and our dog, a corgi we'd raised from a puppy. For Daniel the hardest thing was letting go of his passions for hunting, fishing, and spending time outdoors. Both of us were aware of the relationships and personal comforts we were sacrificing. I also left behind a successful business with an assistant who had been with me for years and was a personal friend.

Daniel and I had been caring for my younger sister, who had diabetes. She needed to be secure before we could move. We originally offered to bring her to Israel, but she was about to enroll in college and didn't think the time was right for her. Bottom line, realizing that we would be so far away was extremely difficult to process.

When I was growing up, my grandfather used to tell me I was Jewish. When the time came for me to tell him about our move, he wished he hadn't told me about my Jewish identity because he did not want me to go. He seemed shocked and upset about the move and could not understand why we would want to live in Israel. Up to that point, I had felt the excitement of the land of Israel being a new adventure and our new home. But that excitement started to mix with the sadness and stress of leaving home and everything familiar. So much was happening so fast that it was easy to lose perspective and overemphasize minor things. Once during our preparation we had a big fight over where to store personal possessions that had real meaning for us. The total process of selling our cars and home, buying tickets, and putting precious things in our lives into storage took three months.

We flew to Israel for only six days, leaving Lily, our daughter, in the care of a friend. In that short time, we had to find an apartment and get everything ready for our return. We ended up securing a small apartment in one of the wildest, most diverse sections of the city, Jaffa, located on the southern border of Tel Aviv, a city of more than four million. Then, on January 11, 2011, we moved into apartment 11.

One of the landmarks in Jaffa is the clock tower in the center of town. In addition to its historical status, the tower seems to beckon the drunken and strung-out late-nighters to find simple carbohydrate sustenance in the famous Abulafia pita bakery, which sells fresh pita breads covered in spices, pizza, or fried eggs by the thousands all day and all night. Our apartment in Jaffa stood just behind one of the busiest areas, near the clock tower square.

Jaffa was undergoing major refurbishment and restoration. The area was destined for investment and improvement with its views of the sea as well as an ancient city attached to it with an elite artists' and restaurant quarter at the seafront. Because of this, there were about five major construction projects near our little apartment. I would awaken at four in the morning to the Muslim call to prayer, and by the time I would finally drift back to sleep, the construction jackhammers would start up at 7 a.m. Adding this layer of sleep deprivation on top of what we were already experiencing with a new baby was just one of the many challenges of our new life in a foreign land.

The early experience of life in this new country and new city was one of culture shock and overstimulation. The Jaffa neighborhood is known for having one of the largest flea markets in Israel, located in a border neighborhood. The area attracted all sorts of drifters and loiterers. We observed thieves and drug deals under our windows at all hours of the night. One night we were sitting on the balcony of our apartment and heard two gunshots. Thinking the noise came from the routine popping of fireworks by local children, we ignored the noise and continued enjoying our drinks. Just a couple of minutes later the phone rang. It was a good friend of ours who lived on Yeffet Street a couple of blocks away. In a panicked voice, our friend told us he'd just witnessed a shooting from the balcony of his home.

Jaffa was also inundated with loud noises around the clock and foul smells due to public urination and poor waste management. Cultural identities meshed. Israelis, Russians, Christians, and Muslims were all our neighbors. Looking out our window, we could see women who were barely dressed while others were fully covered in burkas. At night homeless people would build small fires in the construction sites to stay warm. During the day, the mundane needs of everyday life and survival were a challenge. While shopping for groceries, I had to fight through the aromas of Middle Eastern cooking mixed with the stench of urine and feces. The butcher I went to looked hostile, but I didn't know where else to go.

Daniel felt guilty whenever he took the trash out because we did not have our own dumpster for the building. He would have to walk down the alley behind our home and throw the trash in someone else's can. In Israel this is normal, whereas back in Texas using someone else's dumpster is illegal. These emotions and struggles were compounded even more because very few English speakers live in the Jaffa area. It made us feel lonely and isolated.

This dark and difficult time, compounded by sleep deprivation, brought on a deep depression. "Did we make a mistake by coming here?" I would at times think. But I knew better. The Holy Spirit had given us such clear direction. And as difficult as it was to try to wade through all the challenges, at the end of the day, I would sit on our balcony with its scenic view of the Mediterranean and cry for joy that I was living in Israel. In spite of the struggles, an inner knowing filled me just like it had in my dream. I knew I was living where I was supposed to live. On top of this was the amazing reality that, as a person of Jewish descent, I was living in the place of my inheritance.

We lived in Jaffa for one year and then decided to move out of the intensity of the city. We realized it wasn't Israel that was driving us nuts—it was the city! It wasn't so much the culture shock of Israel but the culture shock of living in an overcrowded, high-energy, fast-paced city. The big-city life was as big of a shock as changing countries.

BE'ER SHEVA

We had a connection through our home in Texas to a couple in Be'er Sheva. Once the ancient home of the biblical patriarch

Abraham, it's a beautiful oasis city located in the desert about sixty miles south of Tel Aviv and forty-five miles from Jerusalem. After visiting the couple in their home, which was in a beautiful, growing suburb, we immediately felt this was the place our family was supposed to be. The single-family homes had yards and gardens with plenty of space with the quiet we needed. It allowed us to do simple and practical things similar to the States, such as being able to park at grocery stores and restaurants without having to walk several blocks. We were even able to find the time to take some Hebrew classes, as life in Be'er Sheva was less demanding.

It was an idyllic suburban life when we moved there, except for the artillery rockets that would fall every week or two. Our first experience with air-raid sirens came early one afternoon while we were cooking dinner together in the kitchen. We scooped up Lily from where she was playing and ran into the bomb shelter. A few seconds later we heard a loud "Boom!" The explosion sent shivers through our bodies as we waited for the signal that it was safe again. The situation in Israel was that Hamas, who rules the Gaza Strip, was receiving and building weapons to launch rockets as far into Israel as they could reach. Part of that reach was the Be'er Sheva area. Rockets were falling within a mile from us, and when they hit, the windows and doors would shake. Yet God filled us with His supernatural grace, and we had no fear. We'd stand outside in peace, watching the rockets fall and knowing they wouldn't come near us.

Part of the Be'er Sheva experience, and even Jaffa, was that we saw the bigger picture. Learning different parts of Israel and some of the unique Israeli culture prepared us for eventually building our life in Jerusalem. The cultures and experiences of Jerusalem are more international. They are full of the influences of tourism from all over but cater to English speakers, mainly from the United States and Canada.

GIVING GOD FULL CONTROL
OF YOUR DESTINY

When we continually make the choice to submit our lives and decisions to God, He becomes the Lord of our destiny. No matter how hard we try to find success in this life, we will never reach our full potential without allowing God to take control. Submitting to the journey is a process that allows us to mature in our walk with Him and brings us to a deeper understanding of His will in the earth.

When Jesus taught His disciples to pray in Matthew chapter 6, He was also teaching them how they could gain vision for the future that God sees.

> Our Father in heaven, hallowed be your name, your kingdom come, your will be done, on earth as it is in heaven. Give us today our daily bread. And forgive us our debts, as we also have forgiven our debtors. And lead us not into temptation, but deliver us from the evil one.
> —MATTHEW 6:9–13

Our hearts are engaged in worship as we lift up the Lord's name as holy in our lives and proclaim that His kingdom will come and His will be done. A heart of worship brings us to a place of clarity where God begins speaking vision into our future. It's in these times that the Holy Spirit fills us up with faith and allows us to see as God sees.

Our faith and deliverance are a result of staying in a worshipful relationship with the Lord. God must bring us to a point of looking at the future as the destiny of His kingdom on earth instead of our destinies as individuals. When we let our own plans for the future go and allow God to set our courses, He will reveal things that we never imagined!

> Remain in me, as I also remain in you. No branch can bear
> fruit by itself; it must remain in the vine. Neither can you
> bear fruit unless you remain in me.
>
> —JOHN 15:4

Life will bring us to many crossroads where we must hear what the Holy Spirit is saying over our direction. "Since we live by the Spirit," wrote Paul, "let us keep in step with the Spirit" (Gal. 5:25). Some decisions won't make sense at the time, but God knows what our next steps are and why those steps are important to establish our faith for the future.

Chapter 2

UNDERSTANDING GOD'S HEART FOR **ISRAEL**

A N INCREDIBLE THING the Lord has shown me is how the future and destiny of a nation is not so different from that of an individual. Looking at us through a father's eyes, God sees our potential before we are ever born. Whether we ultimately fulfill the calling He has over us or mature into the fullness He desires is a matter of our choice to follow Him. The nation of Israel is a prime example of this concept.

> The LORD had said to Abram, "Go from your country, your people and your father's household to the land I will show you. I will make you into a great nation, and I will bless you; I will make your name great, and you will be a blessing. I will bless those who bless you, and whoever curses you I will curse; and all peoples on earth will be blessed through you."
> —GENESIS 12:1–3

When this passage was written in Genesis, Israel was not yet a nation, but God was revealing His heart for a nation to Abraham. Abraham had a choice to follow the call over his life and receive the blessings that came with that call. Abraham did indeed follow God's call and went on to receive many more blessings and ultimately father a nation.

If we look at Israel in the Bible, it doesn't take long to see a pattern emerging of a people who habitually fell away from God and were called back to Him. For most of us this mirrors our own walk with God and the need to continually turn our faces to His will to see our destiny fulfilled. God's relationship with Israel is personal and near to His heart. Scripture tells us that the nation of Israel is the apple of His eye (Zech. 2:8). Below, in Hosea 11, the Lord's relationship to Israel is portrayed as that of a parent and child.

> "When Israel was a child, I loved him, and out of Egypt I called my son. But the more they were called, the more they went away from me. They sacrificed to the Baals and they burned incense to images. It was I who taught Ephraim to walk, taking them by the arms; but they did not realize it was I who healed them. I led them with cords of human kindness, with ties of love. To them I was like one who lifts a little child to the cheek, and I bent down to feed them. Will they not return to Egypt and will not Assyria rule over them because they refuse to repent? A sword will flash in their cities; it will devour their false prophets and put an end to their plans. My people are determined to turn from me. Even though they call me God Most High, I will by no means exalt them. How can I give you up, Ephraim? How can I treat you like Admah? How can I make you like Zeboyim? My heart is changed within me; all my compassion is aroused. I will not carry out my fierce anger, nor will I devastate Ephraim again. For I am God, and not a man—the Holy One among you. I will not come against their cities. They will follow the LORD; he will roar like a lion. When he roars, his children will come trembling from the west. They will come from Egypt, trembling like sparrows, from Assyria, fluttering like doves. I will settle them in their homes," declares the LORD.
>
> —HOSEA 11:1–11

Most of us will face challenges in raising our own children at some point. Despite frustration with our offspring's bad decisions, we would not disown or abandon them. Our heart as a parent is always to see our children make right decisions and reach their full potential.

HOW DO WE FIT IN?

Unfortunately, many in the church today practice varying forms of replacement theology. Replacement theology is rooted in the belief that Israel and the Jewish people are no longer significant to the body of Christ or God's plan in the earth. It is true that most Jewish people in Israel and abroad do not currently believe that Jesus is the Messiah; however, this does not mean that God's plan for Israel has changed.

I first became aware of replacement theology in October of 2010, shortly before moving to Israel. I was sitting in on one of Dad's meetings in Jerusalem when one of the local Messianic leaders brought up replacement theology. I remember being confused and wondering how anyone could believe that Israel had been replaced or that God had abandoned His people with whom He made covenant. Numerous passages in the Bible make it clear that the Jews are God's chosen people and that God maintains a special relationship with the nation of Israel.

> For you are a people holy to the LORD your God. The LORD your God has chosen you out of all the peoples on the face of the earth to be his people, his treasured possession.
> —DEUTERONOMY 7:6

To understand God's plan for us as Gentiles, we must first acknowledge that we have not replaced Israel or the Jewish people. God has extended salvation to Gentiles through the Messiah and brought us into His house as adopted sons.

> In love he predestined us for adoption to sonship through Jesus Christ, in accordance with his pleasure and will—to

the praise of his glorious grace, which he has freely given us
in the One he loves.

—Ephesians 1:4–6

When I made my first trip to Israel, the Lord spoke to me about
how I had been adopted as a Gentile into the promises and destiny of the land. Because I'm the adopted son of my father, Chuck,
it was easy for me to understand this concept of grace and adoption. I was only three days old when I was adopted, so I don't
know much about my birth parents. My family history is the one
God gave me through my adopted family. On that first trip, God
showed me that as believers in Christ our history is the history we
have been adopted into.

If you belong to Christ, then you are Abraham's seed, and
heirs according to the promise.

—Galatians 3:29

In Galatians chapter 3 we can see that through Christ we are
not only linked to the house of Abraham but also heirs to the
promise. If we are heirs to the promise, then our future is linked
to Abraham. One of the Lord's desires is to see the Jewish people
saved and Gentile believers align with them. Remember, Genesis
chapter 12 says those who bless Abraham will be blessed and those
who curse him will be cursed.

Israel is unique in that God's ultimate plan for the nation has
been revealed through biblical prophecy written in the Scriptures.
We know that God's desire is to see Israel and the Jewish people
restored. The Gentiles play a significant role in this restoration
and will step into the promises of salvation through the Messiah.

My personal definition of *vision* is not an understanding of
what God is doing today but a revelation of where He wants to
take us tomorrow. To understand God's will for Israel, we must
allow Him to give us a vision for Jewish and Gentile believers to
move forward as one.

When thinking about prophecy and the role it plays in our

vision for the future, I often turn to the Book of Isaiah. Isaiah knew he had a powerful call over his life to turn the Jewish people back to righteousness. Although it would be generations before many of his prophecies were fulfilled, Isaiah remained faithful to his call. As a result of Isaiah's obedience, today we can look back at his life and see a record of prophetic fulfillment. Seeing the supernatural execution of God's plan through Isaiah should produce faith in us. Faith and prophecy work together, and we must have both if we want to take part in seeing the Lord's will accomplished.

CONVERSATION WITH A JEWISH FRIEND

One day, during a business meeting, I had an interesting conversation with a Jewish friend of mine. Our interaction provides a clear picture of the need for faith in order for this vision to be fulfilled. Shortly after the meeting began, our conversation turned to the Bible and the Jewish concept of the Messiah. He explained that the coming of the Messiah (Savior) has been an eagerly awaited event throughout Jewish history, and almost every generation had someone they thought might be the Messiah.

When you look at the history of the Jewish people, it's not hard to understand why they had such a strong sense of need for a Messiah. Throughout the Bible, Israel fell under the control of various rulers who oppressed the people. Times of extreme hardship and oppression under foreign rule play a prominent role in Jewish history and have shaped Jewish culture and perception.

As the conversation continued, I asked my friend why he did not believe Jesus was the Messiah. He explained that the Jewish people as a whole believe that Jesus could be the Messiah but would not accept Him until He returns to deliver them. One reason many Jews did not follow Jesus as their Messiah in the first century was because He taught of spiritual redemption but had not come to deliver them from the brutal Roman Empire.

We went on to talk about Old Testament prophecy and biblical law. When you engage in this type of conversation with a Jewish person, it is important that you be aware of some cultural things.

In Jewish culture, arguing a point is a way of coming to a collective understanding on a particular subject. When the Bible is discussed, participants in the conversation may argue their points back and forth for hours before a consensus is reached. Although it may just look like an argument to someone who is not familiar with the culture, this is the Jewish and rabbinical way of coming to an understanding. When reflecting on the life of Jesus in the New Testament, one can see that He spent a lot of time debating with the rabbis. Jesus was well respected for His wisdom and understanding, even among those who did not agree with His message. To be an effective witness to the Jewish people, it is critical to develop a strong working knowledge of the Torah.

I asked my friend to explain to me the Jewish understanding of salvation and what he believed concerning admittance into heaven. He explained his belief that the only way to enter heaven was to lead a righteous life and keep biblical and kosher law. My friend admitted that while he had always kept the Ten Commandments (which no one has actually kept, according to Scripture), he was guilty of the occasional breach of kosher law. We had a short laugh before continuing to discuss how difficult it is to truly keep kosher in today's world.

Knowing that I am a Christian, my friend asked my opinion on salvation. I answered that as believers we accept that salvation is by grace and understand that as humans we are incapable of salvation through works. After discussing this concept for a while, I asked my friend whether he had ever known a person he believed had never violated kosher law.

My friend answered that his grandfather had lived a righteous life and had never violated the Torah or kosher law. He went on to tell me his grandfather's story of life during the Holocaust. His grandfather had an opportunity to escape the concentration camps by hiding with Christians who were helping Jewish families escape the Nazis. His grandfather refused to take shelter with the Christians because he knew he would not be able to keep the laws of kosher in their home. As a result of this decision, he was arrested by the Nazis and died in a concentration camp before the war ended.

My friend's story hit me like a ton of bricks. All I could think about was how close this man came to seeing one of the greatest cases of prophetic fulfillment in modern history. If he had only known the grace God had for him, he might have escaped the Holocaust and lived to witness the restoration of Israel as a nation.

Understanding God's grace means understanding that His grace is sufficient for us. There was no way my friend's grandfather could have known Isaiah's words would be fulfilled shortly after the war.

> Do not be afraid, for I am with you; I will bring your children from the east and gather you from the west. I will say to the north, "Give them up!" and to the south, "Do not hold them back." Bring my sons from afar and my daughters from the ends of the earth—everyone who is called by my name, whom I created for my glory, whom I formed and made.
>
> —ISAIAH 43:5–7

You see, God is the One who gives us the ability to see beyond our circumstances and step into grace and fulfillment. He reveals His will through prophecy, but we must not lose sight of the vision He has over our lives.

A NEW WINESKIN FORMING IN THE LAND

Not long ago a friend of mine took me out to lunch in Jerusalem so I could meet one of his colleagues. After the introductions my friend went on to explain that I do some work for my father's prophetic ministry in Texas. As the conversation continued, it quickly became clear that my new acquaintance was skeptical of prophecy and works of the Spirit. In a somewhat condescending way he asked, "So what does God want to tell Israel today?"

After about an hour I left that meeting feeling I had not given a clear answer. Over the next week it continued nagging at me, and I could not shake the feeling that I should have an answer. Several months later the Holy Spirit spoke very clearly and placed it on my heart to read the Bible from cover to cover. Although I have read the entire Bible many times, I don't remember ever reading it straight through. As I began to obey this instruction, the Holy Spirit saturated the room and began imparting to me God's will for the people of Israel in the next generation.

I saw a blending of the old and the new in such a way that it would bring forth a new maturity in the works of the Spirit. God wants to turn the hearts of a younger generation back to the Father and the heart of the fathers back to their children. The Spirit of God said, "A new sound will come out of Israel, and through it I will release My voice into the atmosphere. When this change comes, My people will lift their voices and begin to prophesy to the nations."

As I read through the Scriptures, God revealed a pattern of how the Holy Spirit works. I believe it was important for me to read the Old Testament so I could begin to understand the character of God the Father. It's the Father's desire to see those He raised as children mature into a full relationship with Him. This end has been predestined in heaven and will come! We need to align ourselves with the Holy Spirit if we want to see ancient gates unlocked and the Jewish people reconciled through the Messiah.

Throughout the Bible, someone was always chosen to carry out God's plan and push Israel into the destiny He had ordained. Often those who were anointed were not the ones you might expect. If Saul would not walk in obedience, then David the sheepherder would be anointed king!

When studying the life of King David, it becomes clear that he carried both the physical anointing to the throne of Judah and the spiritual anointing of redemption. The anointing of redemption rested on Ruth the Moabite, who was redeemed in marriage by Boaz and gave birth to Obed. Obed became the father of Jesse and Jesse the father of David.

In 1 Samuel 16 the Lord sent Samuel the prophet to Bethlehem with instructions to anoint one of Jesse's sons king. Upon seeing Jesse's son Eliab, Samuel thought, "Surely the LORD's anointed stands here before the LORD" (v. 6). The Scripture continues:

> But the LORD said to Samuel, "Do not consider his appearance or his height, for I have rejected him. The LORD does not look at the things people look at. People look at the outward appearance, but the LORD looks at the heart."
>
> —1 SAMUEL 16:7

In this story, the Lord is teaching Samuel about recognizing where the anointing rests. Samuel had to learn to see beyond the physical and become one with the heart of God. Like Samuel, it's important for us to learn not to look through the eyes of man and to recognize the move of God. David went on to redeem the throne of Judah, and the Messiah was born out of his family line!

Saul's son Jonathan recognized the anointing that rested on David and was ready to give up the throne in order to see God's redemptive plan come full circle. For Jonathan to align with the move of God, he had to be willing to see past his own personal advancement to the throne and see God's bigger picture.

> And Saul's son Jonathan went to David at Horesh and helped him find strength in God. "Don't be afraid," he said. "My father Saul will not lay a hand on you. You will be king over Israel, and I will be second to you. Even my father Saul knows this."
>
> —1 SAMUEL 23:16–17

Saul's deep desire was to see his son Jonathan become king and take his place on the throne. While a father's desire to see his son receive the inheritance is understandable, Jonathan understood that God's vision for Israel was much larger than man's desire for the throne. As I look back at my own walk with the Lord, I can remember several moments in which the Holy Spirit began to show me what my life and destiny could look like. Our vision for the future is never as large as the potential we have in the Holy Spirit, and the enemy of our souls knows it! The father of lies (Satan) will always stand in conflict with the Spirit of truth.

When we choose to move forward with the destiny God sees over our future, we can expect Satan and his demonic principalities and powers to do everything in their might to suppress or kill the move of God. As you read through the Bible, you can see the strategies Satan employed in an attempt to derail the redemptive plan that rested on David's family line. "For we are not unaware of [Satan's] schemes," wrote Paul in 2 Corinthians 2:11. The enemy has schemes and strategies formed against the plans God has for us.

In 1 Samuel chapter 20, when David received the knowledge that Saul was trying to kill him, he fled the king's presence. After David was absent from the king's table for two days, Saul asked Jonathan why David had not attended the feast. The outburst that followed is a clear example of how Satan will always try to convince us that our future is at stake if we align ourselves with what God is doing!

> Saul's anger flared up at Jonathan and he said to him, "You son of a perverse and rebellious woman! Don't I know that you have sided with the son of Jesse to your own shame and to the shame of the mother who bore you? As long as the son of Jesse lives on this earth, neither you nor your kingdom will be established. Now send someone to bring him to me, for he must die!"
>
> —1 Samuel 20:30–31

You can hear the enemy's voice at work in Saul as he tells his son that his kingdom will never be established unless he chooses to destroy the move of God. To reinforce this point, I want to reference a passage from the life of Jesus. When reading, remember this is the same family line several generations later.

> Therefore many of the Jews who had come to visit Mary, and had seen what Jesus did, believed in him. But some of them went to the Pharisees and told them what Jesus had done. Then the chief priests and the Pharisees called a meeting of the Sanhedrin. "What are we accomplishing?" they asked. "Here is this man performing many signs. If we let him go on like this, everyone will believe in him, and then the Romans will come and take away both our temple and our nation." Then one of them, named Caiaphas, who was high priest that year, spoke up, "You know nothing at all! You do not realize that it is better for you that one man die for the people than that the whole nation perish."
>
> —JOHN 11:45–50

At the time this conversation took place, Jesus was traveling the countryside performing incredible miracles. He had just raised Lazarus from the dead. Why would anyone want to suppress or kill a move like that? As in Saul's day, there were those who sought to keep the throne for themselves rather than aligning with the shift God was making in that season. At the time of Jesus the Sanhedrin acted as a governmental body as well as the ruling religious authority. In hopes of preventing a revolt, Rome had subjected Israel to provincial rule but allowed the Jews to govern themselves.

The Pharisees were so afraid of losing power that they were willing to kill the very move of God in their midst. One of them even acknowledged that Jesus was performing many signs and asked, "What are we accomplishing?" Again, like Saul in 1 Samuel 23, they knew that the anointing had been lifted from them and could see it resting somewhere else. Unable to reconcile this in their minds, they decided to kill Jesus instead of receiving the Messiah they had waited many generations for. In Isaiah we see that this reaction had been prophesied long before:

> Do not call conspiracy everything this people calls a conspiracy; do not fear what they fear, and do not dread it. The LORD Almighty is the one you are to regard as holy, he is the one you are to fear, he is the one you are to dread. He will be a holy place; for both Israel and Judah he will be a stone that causes people to stumble and a rock that causes them to fall.
>
> —ISAIAH 8:12–14

> See, I lay in Zion a stone that causes people to stumble and a rock that makes them fall, and the one who believes in him will never be put to shame.
>
> —ROMANS 9:33

To understand how God's kingdom will be unlocked in the earth, we must first accept that it's not about us or our throne! When we die to ourselves, the move of God starts in our lives.

> Once, on being asked by the Pharisees when the kingdom of God would come, Jesus replied, "The coming of the kingdom of God is not something that can be observed, nor will people say, 'Here it is,' or 'There it is,' because the kingdom of God is in your midst."
>
> —LUKE 17:20–21

If you understand that the kingdom of God is in our midst, then you must come to the conclusion that there is no throne for us to seek in this life. Many of the thrones we set up for ourselves are only illusions and serve to distract us from our destiny. The harder we seek to be enthroned, the more we limit the potential God sees in us. Becoming fixated on our own goals limits what God can do with our future! His plans for us are far greater than anything we can come up with. God desires to unleash our giftings and see us walk in the divine purpose for which we were created.

Would we rather sit in a seat of power for its name's sake or walk in signs and wonders, knowing that our potential has been realized? We can choose to align ourselves with the destiny God sees for us. Acts 13:36 says, "Now when David had served God's purpose in his own generation, he fell asleep." Wow. This should be the goal for all of us—to serve God's purpose in our lives and then go home.

When Jesus came, His life did not resemble what the Jewish people expected from their Messiah. Most believed the Messiah would bring eternal peace and deliver them from the Roman Empire. Spiritual redemption was not what they expected, so when their Messiah did come, many failed to recognize Him. Salvation by grace still eludes the Jewish people and is a stumbling block in Zion! Understanding grace is crucial to understanding redemption! When we accept that we cannot complete God's work in our lives by works, grace begins to take hold of our future.

When grace begins to operate in our lives, we understand our redemption is complete and the Holy Spirit sets a new order in our days. Not only individuals but entire family lines can change course and step into their redemptive purpose. As the Holy Spirit reorders our understanding of redemption, we begin to see our stumbling block as a capstone. This is a perfect illustration. When our vision aligns with God's vision, it allows us to see what He sees. Some things are not by might nor by power but by His Spirit. The Jewish people have an appointed time, and when that time comes, their redemptive purpose will be unlocked!

For generations the Jewish people have tried to attain salvation through works but have not succeeded. Although most practicing Jews have an intense understanding of the Scriptures, they have fallen short of the concept of grace. In Matthew chapter 13 Jesus explains to His disciples that some will see and not perceive, and some will hear and not understand.

> Though seeing, they do not see; though hearing, they do not hear or understand. In them is fulfilled the prophecy of Isaiah: "You will be ever hearing but never understanding;

you will be ever seeing but never perceiving. For this people's heart has become calloused; they hardly hear with their
ears, and they have closed their eyes. Otherwise they might
see with their eyes, hear with their ears, understand with
their hearts and turn, and I would heal them."

—MATTHEW 13:13–15

Still today the focus of Judaism remains the study of Torah
and the belief that salvation can be obtained through keeping the
Law. When Jesus came, His teaching and wisdom—imparted to
Him from the Father—blew that idea to bits. Most of the Jews
couldn't handle it, especially the self-righteous religious leaders.
Likewise, many Christians today are trying to hang on to the law
for their righteousness. As a result they walk in frustration and
failure. If we are going to walk in God's order and His best for
our lives, we must allow Him to bring a complete reversal to our
understanding so we can walk in grace. The law is fulfilled when
we are covered by grace, and true righteousness is the result of
the Holy Spirit working in our lives.

In John chapter 5 Jesus explains that you can study the
Scriptures as diligently as you want and still miss God's plan. If
you are ever seeing and never perceiving, and ever hearing but
never understanding, then it is possible to study the Scriptures
for a lifetime and end up with nothing more than dry religion.

You study the Scriptures diligently because you think that
in them you have eternal life. These are the very Scriptures
that testify about me, yet you refuse to come to me to
have life.

—JOHN 5:39–40

Later, in John chapter 6, Jesus teaches that no one can come to
Him unless the Father draws him or her.

No one can come to me unless the Father who sent me
draws them, and I will raise them up at the last day. It is
written in the Prophets: "They will all be taught by God."

Everyone who has heard the Father and learned from him
comes to me.

—John 6:44–45

When I read the above passage, the Lord began to change my
understanding of how to pray for Israel and the Jewish people.
Not many people know the Father as well as those He raised as
His own. So often in Israel and abroad you can hear the interces-
sors praying into the results of sin and destruction that we can
see with our eyes. It is so important for us to learn to pray the
redemptive will of God instead of only declaring into what we
can see happening around us in the natural.

We are in a time when the Holy Spirit is unlocking spiritual
gifts and setting us on a path that leads to redemption. When a
new order is set based on the Spirit of truth, our governments,
our societies, our families, and our personal lives step into an
open heaven! When the heavens are open over us, we become
one with the Holy Spirit, and the works of Satan have no place
in our midst because the kingdom of God is with us! Wherever
the Spirit of God is poured out, there is no room left for the
enemy to operate because the Holy Spirit fills all the voids left
by human iniquity.

God has placed a burden on my heart to see grace and redemption poured out over Israel. Please join me in lifting up the Jewish
people. God is doing something new in our days! The time is
coming when the Spirit of truth will be unlocked and ancient
gates opened. At the appointed time we won't have to strive to lay
hold of the destiny God sees. That understanding which has been
sealed up and acted as a stumbling stone will be removed!

It is not God's will for some to be ever hearing but never understanding, and ever seeing yet never perceiving. Jesus said that all
who have known the Father and been taught by Him will come to
His Son. Lord, You said that if they would turn, then You would
heal them!

Can you see the power in our intercession when we let the Holy

Spirit unlock our understanding through the Word? We must begin to seek an open heaven over those we want to see redeemed! Remember that the power of life and death is in our tongues, and if we speak from a redemptive anointing, then redemption will come!

> Heaven and earth will pass away, but my words will never pass away.
> —Matthew 24:35

Many of us are experiencing revelation in a way that we never have before. God is mobilizing gifts in people that have long been dormant. He's revealing the meaning of past dreams and visions. Ask the Lord to reveal Himself to you and allow you to see and hear in a new way so that the destiny God sees over your life might be unlocked.

As you join in intercession for the Jewish people, begin to seek an open heaven over the land of Israel. Even if they don't like to admit it, many Jewish people recognize when the truth is spoken. God the Father has woven the truth into them from the beginning, and it has become a part of them! Speak words of redemption, and watch as the truth begins to set people free!

Truth is the key that unlocks the door to understanding, and when our understanding is reversed, the heavens open! Pray that the move of the Holy Spirit will come full circle in Israel and that a new order will be set that allows the supernatural to manifest in the natural. Declare that the move of God will not be missed in this generation and the stumbling stone in Zion will become the capstone!

Chapter 3

DISCERNING THE **TIMES**

S EVERAL YEARS AGO God began placing a burden on my (Daniel's) heart for the education system and had me begin to intercede heavily for the next generation. As the Lord spoke to me about this, He showed me how education is being used to remove discernment from our young people. After this had been on my heart for about a year, I had a disturbing dream that I believe was a warning from the Lord.

In this dream I was arguing with a college professor about the value of his students. The professor insisted that the value of a person was found in his or her knowledge and academic ability. I argued that a person's value is found in his or her God-given drive to succeed and that one's full potential can only be reached when a person finds his or her destiny in Him.

At the end of our conversation the professor was intrigued with what I had to say and asked if I would share my thoughts with his class. In the next part of the dream I found myself standing in a dining room as hundreds of students walked in and sat down around tables. There were three other people who had been asked to address the class before it was my turn to speak. The first person to take the microphone was a college-age girl who spoke for about ten minutes but seemed to have a very plain message that was not striking a chord with anyone. Next, a young man stepped up to the podium, and all he said was "I found Jesus" before falling to the floor as if slain by the Spirit. The whole room seemed to be interested in what was going on but didn't quite know what to make of this.

Just before stepping up to speak, I looked down and realized that I was wearing a long, black robe similar to those worn by Catholic or orthodox priests. Once I was at the podium, the professor met me and began placing several books in front of me. He held up a copy of the Quran and asked me what I knew about it. At that point, I looked down and noticed that the books he'd placed in front of me were from many different religions. In the dream I understood this to mean that he wanted me to convey a message of ambiguity that there are many ways to get to God.

Immediately I took the microphone and began proclaiming that there is only one way to God and sharing the truth of salvation that never changes. I could feel the Holy Spirit rising up in me as I continued to share, but the students were moving around the room, filling their plates with food, and seemed to have lost interest in listening.

SEARCHING FOR A NEW SCHOOL

A few months later Amber and I began searching for a good school to enroll our daughter, Lily, in. She was in the first grade and had attended an American school that did not leave a good impression on our family. We knew there had to be a better choice for her future.

We researched several schools in Jerusalem, and one of them looked promising, so we decided to visit. When we arrived, there was a heavy spirit in the building, and it seemed that the children were downcast. Over the years we have learned that when you feel this type of oppression, there is always some reason for it.

We met with the principal, who introduced himself and began explaining the philosophy and teaching method of the school. He provided us with several books about hands-on learning and offered to take us on a tour of the campus. As we walked the hallways, the conversation turned to religion and how the school handles students with a wide variety of religious beliefs. He explained that the school believes in presenting religion from a historical standpoint and does not endorse any specific religion. As we walked, I did notice that several of the classrooms we visited had pictures of Greek gods and figures from mythology displayed in artwork done by the children.

Before our tour ended, the principal asked whether we wanted to visit the theater arts department and see the students working on an upcoming play. We had plenty of time, so we followed him onto the stage to meet the theater teacher and listen to the kids who were preparing to sing in a musical. As we approached, I noticed that all the children were dressed as figures from Greek mythology. One young boy was wearing a green costume and playing a flute. I turned and asked the principal if this boy was playing the flute of Pan. He smiled and explained that the school was studying Greek mythology and congratulated me on my knowledge of the characters on stage.

For those who are not familiar with Greek and Roman mythology, Pan is a pagan god represented in history as the lord of nature and is well known for his powers of sexual seduction. I remembered visiting Banias in northern Israel, where the remains of a temple to Pan still stands at the mouth of the Jordan River. Ritual sacrifices were thrown into a cave at the site that was thought at the time to be the actual gates of hell.

I couldn't help but wonder whether this was the history these children were being taught, as they were dressed as mythical figures and taught to play the flute of Pan. It grieved my heart to see how young children were unknowingly being placed in a position of worship before a pagan god. This experience opened my eyes to the fact that certain demonic structures are as old as time but continue to manifest in new ways from generation to generation.

We were still curious after leaving the school, so I went home and read part of the book that the principal had given us. As I got deeper into the text, it became evident that the school's philosophy leaned sharply toward secular humanism. It was hard to believe what I was reading because this was exactly what I had seen in my dream. The book explained that the school's teaching philosophy was based on the Greek model of education and value of knowledge.

Secular humanism is rooted in the belief that a person can rely on his own knowledge and abilities, effectively replacing God with human will. While I believe that physical knowledge is a powerful gift from the Lord, it was never intended to replace Him. It might feel more comfortable to trust in our own understanding, but without faith, we miss out on the supernatural knowledge God wants to impart to us.

WHY IT'S IMPORTANT TO DISCERN THE TIMES

Wars have raged since the beginning of time, and our generation has been no exception. As believers it's critical that we understand there is a war taking place around us, a very real war indeed. Yet this war is not for land rights and is not fought with guns and artillery. No, it is for hearts and minds, and it starts when we are young children.

More recently schools in our area have begun sex education programs that introduce lifestyles the Bible clearly defines as sinful. At a young age children are being conditioned to believe the idea that such lifestyles are a valid option and sexuality is a matter of preference.

A good friend of mine has a five-year-old son in the public school system. One day he received a phone call from the principal of the school complaining that his son was throwing a huge fit and was inconsolable. The principal went on to explain that one of the other kids in his class had two parents of the same gender and my friend's five-year-old would not accept it! This reminds me of Jesus teaching His disciples about the faith of children.

> He called a little child to him, and placed the child among them. And he said: "Truly I tell you, unless you change and

become like little children, you will never enter the kingdom
of heaven."

—MATTHEW 18:2–3

Jesus said, "Let the little children come to me, and do not
hinder them, for the kingdom of heaven belongs to such as
these."

—MATTHEW 19:14

Jesus used the innocent faith of children to describe how strong
our faith should be so that we might enter the kingdom of heaven.
My friend's son simply believed the instruction of his parents, who
had led by example in their home with teachings based on the
Word of God.

On another occasion the same friend ran into two of his son's
five-year-old classmates on the sidewalk outside school. As he
started talking to them, one of the boys told him that the two
would be married one day. While trying to keep a straight face,
my friend asked the boys how they were planning to have children.
One of the boys told him not to worry because the couple would
have no trouble finding a surrogate. Having been a youth leader
for many years, my friend was deeply saddened that children who
had not even gone through puberty yet would be knowledgeable
about such things.

As Jesus continued His teaching in Matthew chapter 18, He
made several pointed statements that leave no doubt about how
He views sin and those that would cause children to stray from
the path of life.

If anyone causes one of these little ones—those who believe
in me—to stumble, it would be better for them to have a
large millstone hung around their neck and to be drowned
in the depths of the sea. Woe to the world because of the
things that cause people to stumble! Such things must
come, but woe to the person through whom they come! If
your hand or your foot causes you to stumble, cut it off and

throw it away. It is better for you to enter life maimed or crippled than to have two hands or two feet and be thrown into eternal fire. And if your eye causes you to stumble, gouge it out and throw it away. It is better for you to enter life with one eye than to have two eyes and be thrown into the fire of hell.

—Matthew 18:6–9

Many in today's world would look at these statements and define them as radical or try to redefine them as metaphorical. Make no mistake about it: Jesus was being radical; He was not being metaphorical. He was being real. There is a reason Jesus showed such passion when discussing the importance of ridding our lives of sin. In the next section we take a look at that word *radical* and see how governments and special interest groups have hijacked the term and begun using it to describe anyone who does not agree with their worldview.

When I was growing up, my parents were quite strict about the media they allowed us kids to absorb. My dad would often say that movies, music, and even some popular cartoons contained occult images. He would speak of how certain video games and television shows violated his conscience and would not be allowed in our home. Of course I was convinced my father was being overly sensitive, and I could not understand why many of my friends' parents let them consume the very same media that my parents had restricted. This was frustrating to me, and I felt alienated from my peers who were more influenced by popular culture. However, over the years, as my relationship with the Lord deepened, I have found that the closer I get to His heart, the more sensitive my own conscience becomes.

When observing things through this lens, it becomes clear just how much the bar has been lowered since my early childhood years. I remember watching music videos through the eighties and nineties as they became increasingly suggestive and explicit in nature. Some of the music videos being produced today would have easily been considered pornography a decade ago.

This phenomenon has so entrenched itself in our society that the music itself has suffered in creativity as artists rely on seductive images alone to sell their products. We have become so accepting of these gradual changes that many of today's top artists openly profess satanism as their chosen religion and speak about the strength they gain from personal demons who possess them as they step onto the stage. Yes, we have come a long way since my grandmother used to demonize Elvis for gyrating his hips!

With my own children I find myself researching the integrity of various media outlets in a never-ending attempt to protect their innocence. Any modern parent can tell you that monitoring your children's use of the internet and social media is a full-time job.

Over the last decade an obsession with the occult and supernatural fantasy has taken over the genre of young adult literature and movies. This trend is highly disturbing. Once, when Lily was eight, I took her to one of the schools in Jerusalem for a third-grade placement test. While we were sitting in the lobby, one of the teachers approached and asked Lily what grade she would be going into. After learning that Lily would be attending her class, the teacher asked her what books she enjoyed reading. As the conversation continued, the teacher suggested several popular titles. All of them were based on occult supernatural themes, some of which directly glorified witchcraft.

As we seek the Lord for discernment, we must allow Him to draw the lines in our homes and sometimes we might have a check in our spirits over things that seem as harmless as suggested reading at the local school. Personally I don't have a problem with fictional stories that contain witches and wizards as long as those characters are clearly defined as evil. When witchcraft and the occult are portrayed as harmless, it opens the door to acceptance. Those who are interested in the supernatural may seek demonstrations of power through avenues that God has strictly forbidden. Most will do this without a true understanding of the cost that power comes with.

HOW POLITICS AFFECTS MORAL COMPASS

One of our inherent needs as humans is to find stability in our lives and circumstances. Often, though, our lives feel more like they are vessels being tossed to and fro on rough and choppy waves, with the threat of going under. When pondering this, I am reminded of the process that ships go through while navigating the ocean. Before the availability of GPS, the tools used for navigation needed a fixed position so that the navigator could calculate his location on the water and find the way forward. To complete this process, the navigator needed to know where the stars and constellations would be at the time of year he was planning to sail. He would then use the location of the stars in relation to the horizon in order to determine his whereabouts and plot a course. Likewise, it is necessary for us to know the times and seasons we are living in and have a point of reference that never changes. God's Word never changes, even when the waters and winds of this world pitch and roll all around us! Filled with God's vision as our fixed point of reference, like a good navigator, we can look to the horizon to see what lies beyond.

Eighteen years ago I was certified as an open water scuba diver. It started a life journey that would become a passion. I now have my advanced Open Water Certificate and have been blessed to dive in locations around the world. To pass the test and get a scuba license, one must prove he or she can navigate underwater using only a compass and set landmarks.

On the day of the test I jumped in my instructor's truck, and we made the two-hour trip to a freshwater lake outside Dallas. The lake had formerly been a rock quarry before it was flooded and the water appeared to be crystal clear from the surface. As we suited up, the instructor began explaining how to use the compass while placing a strong emphasis on how important it was to learn navigation properly because the consequences of making mistakes underwater could be deadly. Getting lost underwater means a strong possibility of running out of air!

When I was down in the water, the silt from the bottom of the lake got disturbed and the crystal clear water became so cloudy that I could not see my hands in front of my face. It ended up taking me several tries before I could use the compass to find my way around the different landmarks at the bottom of the lake. Underwater navigation turned out to be the hardest class I would take in becoming certified.

Just as getting lost underwater can be deadly, a navigator of a ship who loses his way could eventually run aground, leading to a shipwreck and the loss of his crew. As we find our way in life, we must allow God to build our discernment and let His Word act as our compass. Even when the water is so murky that we cannot see, God's Word will act as our landmark in times of instability.

In today's atmosphere it can often feel like we are on the ocean and the tide of politics and popular culture are ever changing around us. Over the last several decades we have seen one social revolution after another. Americans have experienced so much change in recent years that no one seems to know where the boundaries of political correctness lie anymore.

We watch as our politicians and elected officials redefine their positions on a daily basis in what seems like a never-ending attempt to keep everybody happy. While some may start out with good intentions, most find out quickly how hard it can be to tell the truth and please everyone. Often during elections voters like to review the record of decisions made by the candidates to determine how truthful they've been throughout their political careers. Understanding this process causes those who operate in the realm of politics to walk a fine line between popularity and the truth.

My life has brought me to a place of belief that our ability to experience freedom is unequivocally linked to the purity of truth that can only be found in the Word of God. Ecclesiastes 3:11 tells us that God has placed eternity in the human heart. This is why nothing in this world will ultimately satisfy except the eternal truth. Even if we don't recognize it, we have a longing built into us to be connected to our Creator, and the way we connect with Him is through the truth of His Word. "In the beginning was the

Word," wrote John, "and the Word was with God, and the Word was God" (John 1:1). To know God is to know His Word. Every human being has God's truth woven into his or her being.

No matter what kind of life a person is living, his or her internal spirit recognizes when the truth is spoken. Isaiah told us that God's Word will not return void and will accomplish its purpose. Every human being has a God receptor built inside him or her. This is why intellectual arguments are not as effective as simply speaking God's Word. Because God created us in His image, we are conduits for the Spirit of truth in the earth. Most of the time, He moves through humans to humans. Knowing this, Satan works incredibly hard to drown out the voice of truth in our lives. We can't allow him a foothold! In our walk with the Lord we should make no attempt to redefine God's Word or apologize for what it says. The quickest way we can lose the Word of God is by allowing others to define it for us in a way that suits any agenda other than God's intended purpose—to set us free.

Over the years I have watched as politicians, special interest groups, and the court system have systematically made decisions to remove God's Word from our society. For those in the United States who are interested in a brief history, our Supreme Court made several landmark decisions in the early 1960s that effectively removed prayer and the Bible from our public schools. More recently there have been decisions to remove replicas of the Ten Commandments from all public buildings on the basis that honoring the Bible violates the religious freedom of nonbelievers.

Much of the confusion surrounding the last several decades in American politics can be directly traced to the removal of God's Word from the public schools. On a social level this has led to a national identity crisis. If we continue to adopt a false narrative, Satan will gain an even stronger foothold in the personal lives of many, especially our children.

Another disturbing trend is the recent political push to remove statues of historical figures associated with the American Civil War from public buildings. In addition, there is a strong political push to change not only the Bible but the history books as well. If history has taught us anything it's that as soon as we fail to honor it, we will repeat it.

As we saw earlier, the truth is something we recognize in our spirits. Even the law of man finds its base in God's Word. I believe this is because those who originally wrote it were convicted by the same truth. As a student in the police academy I studied Texas criminal law intensively. One of the classes involved the section of the penal code dealing with violent crime. Studying the different offenses, it was undeniably clear to me how closely the wording in some of these statutes resembled the Bible. Seeing firsthand how God's Word had been used as the basis for many of our laws left a deep impression on me.

When we covered the law of murder in our books, the instructor went through chapter 19 of the penal code explaining what constitutes the various charges for criminal homicide in Texas. The last sentence of the statute defined an exception:

> This chapter does not apply to the death of an unborn child if the conduct charged is:...a lawful medical procedure performed by a physician or other licensed health care provider with the requisite consent, if the death of the unborn child was the intended result of the procedure.[1]

The instructor went on to explain how the laws governing homicide had to be altered to accommodate abortion after the Supreme Court's landmark decision in the *Roe v. Wade* case of 1973. My purpose in discussing the issue of abortion is to illustrate how the law had to be altered to accommodate the agenda of special interest groups. We need to remember that not all special interests come from the Lord, and many are not even accepted by the majority.

CHANGING TIMES AND LAWS

Daniel chapter 7 talks about how the beast will attempt to change the law and set times in the earth. Accepting God's law as a benchmark and basis for our decrement is key to understanding how God works in time.

As this assault on biblical truth continues to be driven by those who would try to redefine the law, we are increasingly left in a state of confusion concerning morality. When *Roe v. Wade* passed, the issue was no longer "Thou shalt not kill" but "What constitutes life?" What was once clearly and simply defined as sin now sinks into ambiguity and begins to raise more questions than answers.

You can look at many other issues in the law and see the same principle at work. As laws that were based in divine truth are altered, it inevitably leads to more questions than answers. The fallout of this redefining of truth is evident all around us today as the next generation begins to question their identities, even to the point of viewing their genders as a choice.

Over the years I have watched many around me struggle with issues of identity for various reasons. One thing is certain, though: confusion over issues of identity is one of the strongest tools Satan uses to replace the truth we have in Christ. Wherever we suffer from identity crisis, Satan rushes to fill us with counterfeits because he knows that God desires to fill us up with His authentic purpose and vision. To change the identity of a person or a nation, the existing foundation must first be destroyed. The father of lies will stop at nothing to redefine truth and alter our laws to the point that they no longer reflect the Word of God.

In Romans chapter 2 we find a clear picture of our accountability to uphold the letter of God's law, but more importantly, the intent of the law. The conscience of those who live by the Spirit of truth will bear witness and cause them to have discernment even in the absence of the written Word of God.

> All who sin apart from the law will also perish apart from the law, and all who sin under the law will be judged by the

law. For it is not those who hear the law who are righteous in God's sight, but it is those who obey the law who will be declared righteous. (Indeed, when Gentiles, who do not have the law, do by nature things required by the law, they are a law for themselves, even though they do not have the law. They show that the requirements of the law are written on their hearts, their consciences also bearing witness, and their thoughts sometimes accusing and at other times even defending them.) This will take place on the day when God judges people's secrets through Jesus Christ, as my gospel declares.

—ROMANS 2:12–16

In Jeremiah chapter 31 Jeremiah is prophesying to Israel about the new covenant and how there will come a time when God will place His law on their minds and write it on their hearts.

"The days are coming," declares the LORD, "when I will make a new covenant with the people of Israel and with the people of Judah. It will not be like the covenant I made with their ancestors when I took them by the hand to lead them out of Egypt, because they broke my covenant, though I was a husband to them," declares the LORD. "This is the covenant I will make with the people of Israel after that time," declares the LORD. "I will put my law in their minds and write it on their hearts.

"I will be their God, and they will be my people. No longer will they teach their neighbor, or say to one another, 'Know the LORD,' because they will all know me, from the least of them to the greatest," declares the LORD. "For I will forgive their wickedness and will remember their sins no more."

—JEREMIAH 31:31–34

In the days to come, this war over the hearts and minds of the culture will be won by having the Word of God written on our hearts. As we walk through life, most will come to an understanding that those things the Bible defines as sin inevitably lead to death. Without going too far into a political discussion, we need to understand as believers that the atmosphere around us is changing at breakneck speed, and we can't bow to every worldly agenda and hold fast to the truth that is our freedom.

Ministers must hold fast to the truth.

Chapter 4

WAR **WEARY**

A MERICA WILL NEVER forget the day terrorism became a reality in the West. About a week before September 11, 2001, my training with the Denton County Sheriff's office started. I'll never forget the look of shock on my sergeant's face when he walked into our classroom and announced the tragedy at the World Trade Center. Our class of thirty recruits crowded around a small television just in time to see the second plane crash. A sinking feeling formed in the pit of my stomach as the reality hit me that America would never be the same and that we were going to war. Several of the recruits I worked with quit their jobs and joined the military shortly after the 9/11 attacks.

Within weeks the CIA started conducting operations on the ground in preparation for a full-scale invasion of Afghanistan. Over the next decade, the United States went to war with Saddam Hussein in Iraq and began a campaign of drone strikes that involved several Middle Eastern countries.

After the 9/11 attacks, almost immediately there was a strong backlash in the media. Muslim religious figures started appearing on talk shows and news outlets asserting that Islam is a religion of peace. Influential Muslim leaders attempted to define *jihad* as an inner struggle rather than a physical war against unbelievers. Non-Muslim populations living in North Africa or the Middle East are likely to tell you a very different story.

UNDERSTANDING ISLAM IN THE MIDDLE EAST

Since 2001 the American consciousness of Islam and terrorism has grown considerably. We were again shocked in February of 2002 when a video was released showing the decapitation of American journalist Daniel Pearl at the hands of masked terrorists. During this time, most Americans were becoming aware that we had enemies in the East with deep religious convictions who were capable of extreme acts of cruelty.

To understand what it's like to live with the threat of terrorism in Middle Eastern countries, you first need a basic knowledge of Islam. In traditional Islamic culture there is little separation of church and state. Hard-line Muslims believe that Islamic law, called Sharia law, should be the basis for governmental law. Organizations such as the Muslim Brotherhood in Egypt form because the existing government is unwilling to implement Sharia. If one of these organizations manages to gain control and implement Sharia law, then Muslim religious figures end up in positions of power because they define the law.

When there is a bombing in the Middle East, we often ask why Muslims are blowing up other Muslims. In some countries terrorist organizations do not have the military resources to overthrow the government they perceive as secular or westernized. These organizations rally many to their cause through a call for the return to fundamental Islam and implementation of Islamic law. If hard-line Islamic groups are not able to gain control over the government through political means, they will engage in armed resistance that may go on for years. In this war civilian casualties are looked at as martyrs in the cause of Allah.

Before accepting Islam as a religion of peace, consider that Muhammad himself first brought Islam to Mecca by way of the sword. By the time Muhammad died in the year AD 632, he had conquered most of the Arabian Peninsula in the name of Allah. Muslim caliphs who succeeded Muhammad continued the spread of Islam through conquest.

After the death of Muhammad a disagreement arose over who

should be his successor. A majority of Muslims chose to follow Muhammad's close friend Abu Bakr. They became known as Sunnis. Muslims who chose to follow Muhammad's son-in-law Ali became the Shia. There are other smaller sects of Islam today, but understanding Shia and Sunni differences is key to Middle East politics.

Syria has become the most recent battleground in the Sunni versus Shia conflict. Both the Sunni and Shia have a strong interest in who controls Syria. President Bashar Al-Assad finds some of his government's closest allies in Iran, a stronghold of the Shia. Opposing rebel forces are largely made up of Syria's majority Sunni population. Iran and its Shia proxy, Hezbollah (a Shia Islamist political party and militant group), support Assad, while Sunni nations support the rebels.

When a war such as this one occurs, sympathizers from neighboring countries often cross the border and fight for one side or the other. Combatants on both sides will claim they are fighting a holy war in the name of Allah. When this happens, it creates the strong possibility that a larger, regional war could follow.

In modern times terrorism has been characterized as a brand of asymmetric and unpredictable warfare that is often fought on multiple fronts. This war of insurgency and attrition has little or no respect for borders and should be looked at as a regional rather than localized issue. We must recognize this in the West if we wish to win wars in the Middle East. Passages in the Quran dictate that nonbelievers should pay a tax to the Muslims, be expelled from Muslim lands, or be killed for refusing to convert to Islam. I am encouraged, however, that our understanding of the Middle East will continue to grow as a generation of soldiers returns from Iraq and Afghanistan.

THE PALESTINIAN CONFLICT

As Amber wrote about earlier, when our family first moved to Israel in January of 2011, we settled in the city of Jaffa on the outskirts of Tel Aviv. Jaffa was an Arab city prior to the establishment of Israel in 1948 and remains predominantly Arab today. Our second-story apartment was located in the last Jewish neighborhood bordering Jaffa.

One day about a month after we moved in, I left the apartment to find a SWAT team dressed in riot gear at the end of our street. As I approached the famous clock tower in downtown Jaffa, I could see protesters waving the Palestinian flag as they marched down Yefet Street. By the end of the day, numerous protesters had been arrested and several police officers injured. This scenario would repeat itself several more times during our stay in Jaffa, but this particular day marked our first experience with the Palestinian conflict.

Before the 1948 War of Independence in Israel, the Arab people who occupied the region collectively referred to themselves as Palestinians. When the war started, a large number of these people fled the land that is now Israel and went to neighboring countries. At the time, most Arabs believed that regional powers would quickly regain the land and they would return to their homes within weeks. To their shock and dismay, Israel supernaturally won the war, and a Jewish state was created instead.

All the Arab people who stayed in Israel through the war were given Israeli citizenship. People who fled to neighboring countries were refused citizenship upon their return. Since 1948 none of the surrounding countries have extended citizenship to the Arabs who left during the war, leaving them to be defined as refugees indefinitely. Politics plays a big part in the Palestinian problem, as naturalizing a large population would shift the political structure of any of these countries, including Israel.

Arab people defining themselves as Palestinians now make up a majority of the population in the West Bank, Jordan, and Gaza. Using the word *refugee* is a bit misleading to us in the West because we think of refugees as living in tent communities under substandard conditions. In Israel most cities in the West Bank and Gaza closely resemble those in the rest of the country. On the ground there is a difference between Arabs who are Israeli citizens and those who define themselves as refugees. Terrorist organizations such as Hamas have traditionally sprung up from inside the populations who are not Israeli citizens. Cities that are made up of Israeli Arabs tend to have fewer problems with terrorism.

Being led of the Holy Spirit on a daily basis is critical. Over here we can't afford to let our guard down spiritually or physically. Allowing the Lord to set our course, along with learning to recognize dangerous situations, has become an important part of our lives. Living in Israel means learning to deal with the constant spiritual tension and threat of terrorism. Islam is a major stronghold, and almost anywhere you go in the country, you will have Muslim neighbors. Although living with these threats has not always been easy, it has increased our faith and strengthened our relationship with the Lord.

OUR PERSONAL EXPERIENCES WITH ROCKETS

In December of 2011 our family moved from Jaffa and settled near the city of Be'er Sheva. Be'er Sheva is located in southern Israel about twenty miles from the Gaza Strip. After seeking God over this move, we felt strongly that He wanted us positioned in this area for the next season. Many of our friends in Tel Aviv could not understand why anyone would want to move to the south, where rockets are a problem.

Since 2001 terrorist groups in Gaza have fired over ten thousand artillery rockets and mortar shells into southern Israel.[1] At times this ongoing barrage has made life in southern communities almost unbearable. Hamas and other terrorist organizations use rockets in the belief that they will eventually drive the Jews out of Israel. While this may seem ridiculous to some, Hamas is emboldened by terroristic tactics that have succeeded in overturning governments in the past. Over the years this campaign of violence has been defined as a Palestinian resistance to Jewish occupation. Hamas made it clear in their charter that resistance will not end until all perceived Palestinian lands are liberated.[2] Understanding this is important when considering a two-state solution to the Palestinian problem. As long as the Jewish state exists, organizations such as Hamas will not end their resistance.

Our family's first experience with a rocket attack happened about three months after we moved south. Our family was in the kitchen preparing to cook dinner when the alarm sirens sounded. Amber ran to get Lily from the living room, where she was playing, and the three of us crowded into our bomb shelter. Several seconds after the alarm ended, we heard a loud explosion that shook the house. Later, Israeli news reported that a Grad rocket had been fired from Gaza and exploded near the city of Be'er Sheva.

Most houses in Israel are made of cement and have one room that is reinforced with a heavy door and metal plating on the windows. In our home we gave the safe room to our daughter, Lily, so we would not have to wake her up when forced to take shelter at night. In Be'er Sheva the warning time is around one minute between hearing the siren and the rocket's impact. Some of the towns and farming communities closer to Gaza have as little as fifteen seconds.

Hamas and other organizations in Gaza use four types of projectiles to terrorize southern communities in Israel. Heavy mortar shells are fired from a tube and have a range of around six miles. Mortar shells are often fired at Israel Defense Forces (IDF) troops as well as civilians on or near the Gaza border. Qassam rockets are manufactured in Gaza and were named after the Hamas military wing, the Izz ad-Din al-Qassam Brigades. Rocket makers often use piping taken from road signs or other sources to make Qassams, which have a range of eleven miles.

Grad rockets are military-grade artillery rockets with a medium range of twenty-five miles. Grads were originally designed in Russia and intended to be fired from a truck-mounted launcher. These rockets are nine feet in length and carry about sixty pounds of explosives along with the ball bearings often added to increase destructive capabilities. Grad-type rockets are now produced in numerous countries, including China and Iran. Several variants of this weapon have been smuggled into Gaza for use against Israel.

Iranian-made Fajr-5 rockets are believed to be the longest of the long-range weapons possessed by Hamas. Fajr-5 rockets are the size of a telephone pole and carry an explosive charge around three hundred pounds. These rockets have a range of fifty miles and were first deployed against Israel in November of 2012 during Operation Pillar of Defense.

There is little difference between rockets and missiles except that a missile has a guidance system and rockets do not. The use of rockets in this context is a true act of terrorism, as the person who fires it has little or no control over where it will land. Roadside bombs and anti-tank missiles are also commonly used against IDF troops as they patrol the borders of Gaza. Southern communities have been known to experience rocket fire about every two weeks, even in times of relative peace. Militants in Gaza conduct random launches just to remind Jewish residents they are not welcome here. There are several terrorist organizations in Gaza, including Islamic Jihad and other groups, some of whom are al-Qaeda affiliates. Hamas is the official government in Gaza, so they often deny responsibility for these attacks and place the blame on smaller organizations.

In 2012 there were three major escalations in the Gaza conflict leading up to operation Pillar of Defense. Escalations usually occur when someone is killed in a terror attack emanating from Gaza or an Israeli air strike aimed at stopping such attacks. Israel's targeted assassinations against the leaders of Hamas and other organizations also tend to spark hostilities. Most of these escalations last about a week and see the firing of several hundred rockets as well as retaliatory air strikes by the IDF.

When an escalation occurs, southern Israel quickly goes from a low grade of conflict to all-out war. Life changes considerably in times of war. Businesses and schools are closed, and most people stay in their homes or near a safe room. Sleep deprivation also becomes a problem when rockets are fired at all hours of the night for several days. Most people we know keep their homes stocked with enough food and water to last for a couple of weeks should supplies become scarce. Israel also provides gas masks to its residents to protect against biochemical attacks.

One night, Amber and I had friends visiting from Jerusalem who had never experienced a rocket attack. At three o'clock in the morning we had two alarms back to back, and all four of us had to take shelter in Lily's room. The next day, we were eating at our favorite restaurant in Be'er Sheva when the alarms sounded again. The kitchen was the safest room in the building, so we crowded in with the cooks and waitresses until the danger had passed.

Occasionally I have found myself in situations where an attack occurred and there was no access to a bomb shelter. One day, while we were in a taxi on the way to the bank in Be'er Sheva, the alarms sounded. The driver immediately pulled over and motioned for me to follow him. We ran to the door of the nearest building, but the security guard refused to let us in. The cab driver was an elderly Jewish man and was visibly shaken. As traffic came to a stop at a nearby intersection, a Palestinian rolled down his window and began yelling, "I am not afraid. The bomb is not for me." This is an example of callous Middle East humor. After the rocket exploded, we returned to the taxi and went about our day.

Over a million people live in cities near Gaza and must deal with this threat on a daily basis. Northern Israel briefly experienced a similar situation during the Second Lebanon War with Hezbollah in 2006. Over the last decade, rockets have killed or injured hundreds and caused untold property damage. Most countries would not put up with such an indiscriminate attack on their civilians!

OPERATION PILLAR OF DEFENSE

Operation Cast Lead ended in January of 2009, marking the beginning of a tense three years in the Gaza conflict. Militants used the time to rearm and acquire more-sophisticated weapons.

Rocket fire lulled shortly after the war, but with a renewed call to jihad, it soon resumed.

Hamas has enjoyed increased political support since the Arab Spring succeeded in removing Egyptian president Hosni Mubarak in 2011. After the fall of Mubarak, the Muslim Brotherhood gained control of the government in Egypt, and their candidate, Mohamed Morsi, was elected president. Hamas and the Muslim Brotherhood share the same ideology and have close political ties. As more regional leaders lose power to the Arab Spring, they are likely to be replaced by those sympathetic to Hamas and the Palestinian cause.

Israel saw a marked increase in violence in the weeks and months leading up to Operation Pillar of Defense. In the fall of 2012, soldiers were routinely attacked while carrying out patrols along the Gaza border. Roadside bombs and sniper fire became an almost normal occurrence by mid-October.

Israelis were outraged on November 10 when terrorists in Gaza fired an anti-tank missile, destroying an IDF jeep on the Israeli side of the border. Four soldiers were injured in the attack, one of them seriously.[3] Helicopters evacuated the wounded to a medical center in Be'er Sheva, right down the street from our home. After that, public opinion began to shift as it became clear that a wider Gaza conflict was unavoidable.

Four days later the IDF officially kicked off Operation Pillar of Defense with the stated goal of putting a stop to rocket fire and restoring calm to the south. Ahmed Jabari, head of the Hamas military wing, was killed by an Israeli air strike in the opening hours of the campaign.

Within an hour after Jabari was killed, we received phone calls from friends all over the country warning us that things were about to get bad in our area. It wasn't long before the first alarms sounded and sent us running for the bomb shelter. After counting eighteen explosions in that first attack, we realized this wasn't going to be the same as the smaller ones we had experienced in the past.

Israel immediately launched air strikes targeting the underground stockpiles of long-range rockets in Gaza. Government officials announced on November 15 that they believed most of the Iranian-made Fajr-5 rockets had been destroyed in the first round of bombings. Terrorists launched over two hundred rockets into southern Israel in the first twenty-four hours of the operation. Israel continued its air campaign targeting Hamas infrastructure and rocket launching squads.

One night, we attended a wedding party at a friend's house in our neighborhood. About half an hour after the party started, we could faintly hear the sound of alarms going off over the music. There were eighty people at the party, so there wasn't room in the shelter for everyone. Amber and I joined several of our friends in the front yard to watch the action. I will never forget how surreal it felt to look up at the night sky and see those orange balls of light zipping over the city. Moments later, several loud explosions reminded us that they were not fireworks!

The next day, I went to Ben Gurion University in Be'er Sheva to pick up a friend. Just as I was loading her suitcase into the trunk of my car, the alarm sirens began again. With no shelter in the area, we ran to the nearest building and took refuge near a brick wall. Israel's Iron Dome missile-defense system fired three Tamir interceptors high into the air above our heads. We watched as the interceptors destroyed several incoming Grad rockets, leaving a thick trail of white smoke in their wake. Despite the danger in this situation, I have to say it was one of the most incredible things I have ever seen.

Two Fajr-5 rockets were fired at Tel Aviv on November 15, setting off the alarm sirens for the first time since the 1991 war.[4] Tel Aviv residents were shocked by the event, as many had long considered themselves out of range in the Gaza conflict. Jerusalem also went through this realization as several of these rockets were fired at the city in the days that followed.

Only one of the long-range rockets hit inside a major city, while the rest were intercepted or fell outside populated areas. The final rocket destroyed the top floor of an apartment building in Rishon LeZion near Tel Aviv. Most of the building's residents made it to the safe room before the blast. Two people were hospitalized after being lightly injured by falling debris. Over seventy thousand reserves were called up in the first three days of fighting as IDF troops lined the borders of Gaza in preparation for a ground offensive. Several of our friends from Tel Aviv received orders to pack their things and report to bases for duty.

One afternoon we stopped at a gas station on Highway 6 near our home. Armored personnel carriers and trucks carrying tanks were parked along the shoulder of the highway and took up most of the parking lot. There was an air of national pride inside the gas station as young soldiers prepared themselves to make sacrifices defending their country. The older men wore a look of concern, as some of them had undoubtedly seen combat before. Almost everyone in Israel has friends or family members actively serving in the military, so this was an emotional time for the whole country. Military service is mandatory, and the population here understands the dangers associated with an incursion into the Gaza Strip.

One of our friends from Tel Aviv found out his wife was pregnant just before receiving orders to report for duty. We spent a lot of time praying for him, as his specialty as an explosives ordnance technician is one of the more dangerous jobs in the military. After spending years in law enforcement, I know firsthand about clearing a house not knowing whether there are armed subjects inside. One of our friends who spent some time in Gaza explained that parts of the city are like a maze, and Hamas would use an array of explosives and booby traps to deter advancing troops.

As the conflict raged on for several days, we began to understand what people mean when they say the fog of war. I have experienced tense situations in the past, but the spiritual and physical intensity of warfare is something you can hardly describe. One of the hardest realizations we came to was that our friends and family would never truly be able to relate to some of these experiences.

Around midday on November 21, while inside a store in Be'er Sheva, I saw on the news that something bad had happened. A city bus had been bombed in Tel Aviv. The steady stream of Hebrew in the background became a blur as people in the store gathered around the TV to stare at pictures of the charred bus and medical personnel removing the injured. Emotions in the room quickly turned to anger and frustration as the images brought back memories of the Second Intifada Palestinian uprising. An Egyptian-brokered ceasefire went into effect later that evening, bringing Operation Pillar of Defense to an abrupt end. Public support for a ground operation was at its height after the bombing, and most Israelis believe that Hamas will continue to pose a security threat in the future.

THE AFTERMATH OF WAR

After the war ended, we experienced some mixed emotions. It took some time to process our remorse for those who had been killed and the knowledge that the ceasefire was only a temporary solution.

Although the war was a traumatic experience for our family, the Lord knew how to use this situation to open doors that otherwise might not have been opened. Over the next several months we watched as God began to use these experiences to strengthen our walk for the future. Little did we know that we would soon have several chance encounters with our neighbors from Gaza.

MEETING THE ENEMY FACE TO FACE

While on our annual trip home to Texas, Amber and I decided to take a short vacation to the Caribbean. When we boarded the return flight, Amber was drawn to a young woman and her two children sitting in the aisle behind us. As the two struck up a conversation, Amber noticed that her kids seemed to know the drill and asked if their family traveled much. The woman answered that she made international trips often but was hesitant to give any details. As the conversation continued, she revealed that her family was from "Palestine" and she made frequent trips to Gaza to visit them.

Amber told her that we had lived in Israel for two years and were currently staying in Be'er Sheva near the Gaza Strip. The woman went on to tell us about her family and the hardships of life in Gaza. She explained that her family hates Israel and feels that the Israeli occupation is responsible for poor living conditions in Gaza. She also told us that some of her brothers and cousins were involved with Hamas and would often go out to fire rockets! In that moment, we realized that this person we were talking to had direct ties to terrorism. I could almost hear the air raid sirens all over again as her face became the face of all our sleepless nights. We continued talking to her, even though deep inside it was hard to suppress feelings of anger.

About that time, I noticed that the woman had several male relatives sitting a few rows behind us who were just out of earshot but seemed very interested in our conversation. I could feel their thoughts and see it in their eyes: "What is she doing talking to this American, and why is she telling them all about our lives?" By that point, we strongly sensed that the Lord had placed this woman in our path for a reason. Later in the flight the woman began to question Amber about her life and what she believes. Her eyes began to fill up with tears as Amber shared about her personal relationship with Jesus. The concept of a God that loved her was not something this woman had ever experienced before. The Holy Spirit was drawing her as she began to process what she was hearing. By the time we got off the plane in Dallas, this woman's life had been touched by the Lord, and she would not forget the experience. Who knows how the Holy Spirit would water the seeds that were planted inside her. The Word of God never comes back void.

For us this chance encounter was an opportunity to see a face behind the mask of Islam. It was important for us to see our neighbors as human instead of simply our enemies. While Islam is indeed the enemy of both Christians and Jews, we must remember that there are millions of Muslims who live their lives under tremendous spiritual oppression. Most have never experienced the love that Jesus has for them!

HEALING IN OUR HOME

Some months later I got a phone call from a friend of mine who lives near Gaza. He informed me that he would be in our neighborhood the next day and asked if he could bring a pastor from Bethlehem and his parents to meet us in our home. He further explained that his friend's parents live in Gaza and are only allowed into Israel once a year for Christmas. After hanging up the phone, Amber and I discussed how interesting it was that God was bringing residents of Gaza into our home.

Our guests arrived around 1 p.m. the following afternoon. After serving tea and coffee, we sat down in the living room, and the pastor from Bethlehem began to share his testimony. He told us how the Holy Spirit had met with him while he lived in Gaza and how he could not stop sharing the truth about Jesus with others. His obedience to God's call over his life placed him in direct conflict with the Muslim majority in Gaza. Not long before his life fell under intense attack, one of his close friends was martyred. The pastor continued to share the gospel, but it became evident that he would not survive for long in Gaza. Eventually he moved to Bethlehem, where the Lord has graciously allowed him to continue sharing the truth with the Palestinian people.

After hearing his testimony, we had an opportunity to get to know his parents, who are Christians currently living in Gaza. They did not speak much English, so the pastor translated for us in Arabic. Our new friends spent some time telling us what it means to be a believer in Gaza and graciously shared many of their personal experiences.

As our conversation progressed, we began to discuss the war and how it affected our lives on both sides. Amber and I told them how we would lie in bed at night listening to the explosions in Gaza and pray for those who had been injured and their families.

We recounted our experience of how the Iron Dome had protected the city and how surreal it had been to watch missiles flying over our neighborhood.

Our new friends' eyes filled up with tears when they saw that our bomb shelter was Lily's room and began to apologize for the rockets that had been fired into Israel. They further explained that most in Gaza were not living in fear during the war because they know that Israel takes great care not to hit civilian targets. Although explosions had shaken their home, they never lost power or basic utilities.

Before our friends left, we spent some time in prayer for both Israel and the Palestinian people. God used our meeting with this couple to bring healing into our home and show us how to pray for those from Gaza who stand with us in the body of Christ. If I took anything away from our experiences that day, it was that even in the midst of our enemies, we find those God is reaching out to. In the end we are united through our faith in the Messiah and the truth that never ends!

ENGLISH LESSONS IN RAHAT

When the Lord heals you, He will often call on you to take part in the healing of others.

In January of 2013 a friend of mine who worked with Ben Gurion University called and asked me to take part in a project she was working on. For several years she had been teaching English classes in the city of Rahat as part of an after-school program. Rahat is one of several Bedouin settlements located in southern Israel. The Bedouin people are an Arab people group who were traditionally nomadic and have only recently begun to settle in modern cities. The Bedouin still face many hardships associated with this dramatic change of lifestyle, and learning English is one thing that can open doors to them in education.

Formerly the class was held in a designated building, but it had been moved to one of the local mosques due to lack of resources. My friend did not feel entirely secure about the change of venue, so she was more than happy to have me sign on as an assistant. Based on prior years of experience, we expected around twenty children to participate in the program. When we arrived to teach the first class, there were around fifty waiting for us! My friend decided to split the children into four groups, with each of us teaching two classes. My first class consisted of ten kids between the ages of six and eight. The second class was between eight and twelve. While teaching in Rahat, I was blessed to build friendships with many of the children as well as the program coordinator, Jihad. I had met Jihad once before when we had gone to his father's house to purchase our Passover lamb the year prior.

After teaching for several weeks, my friend informed me she had been speaking to several interns who were interested in assisting our efforts in Rahat. The following week, we stopped at the university and picked up two young ladies on our way out of town. Shortly into our conversation we found that one of them had moved to Be'er Sheva only two weeks before the war started. Her husband worked for the US military and was away from home for most of the conflict. She soon confided that her short stay in Israel had been incredibly traumatic, and that it was hard for her to look at Arab people as anything other than her enemies.

As she took part in the lesson that night, her perception started to change. She stood quietly in the corner of the room while the children ran around smiling and playing games. When the evening came to an end, she walked out of the classroom, looking a little less traumatized then when she had arrived. On the ride home she opened up to my friend and told her how meeting the Bedouin children had allowed her to see them as human beings and how she felt that some of the trauma from the war had been lifted from her shoulders.

I went on to teach English in Rahat for several more months and grew to love the children. The majority of Muslims in the Middle East are taught from a young age that Americans and Western culture are enemies of Islam and are the cause of most of their problems. Any opportunity to interact with these children and let them see the love that God has for them is a step toward peace.

LEARNING TO WALK IN VICTORY

Throughout our experiences the Lord has indeed taught us to walk in victory! While Israel goes through seasons of war and peace, the one thing that remains steadfast and true is that God's gifts and callings are irrevocable.

Throughout the Bible there are verses that point to God as Israel's strength in battle, but how does that apply to us today and how can we learn to walk in victory in our daily lives? I love the following passage in Romans because it reflects the current state of Israel and ends with the statement that God's gifts and His call are irrevocable.

> I do not want you to be ignorant of this mystery, brothers and sisters, so that you may not be conceited: Israel has experienced a hardening in part until the full number of the Gentiles has come in, and in this way all Israel will be saved. As it is written: "The deliverer will come from Zion; he will turn godlessness away from Jacob. And this is my covenant with them when I take away their sins." As far as the gospel is concerned, they are enemies for your sake; but as far as election is concerned, they are loved on account of the patriarchs, for God's gifts and his call are irrevocable.
> —ROMANS 11:25–29

The ability to see God's gifts and call at work in our lives is the first step to walking in His fullness. Victory becomes a way of life for us when we step into the irrevocable call that God predestined. It is possible to ignore the call God has over your life, but if you choose to follow Him, there is no end! In Isaiah chapter 9 it was prophesied that the Messiah would be born to the throne of David and there would be no end to the greatness of His government and peace.

For to us a child is born, to us a son is given, and the government will be on his shoulders. And he will be called Wonderful Counselor, Mighty God, Everlasting Father, Prince of Peace. Of the greatness of his government and peace there will be no end. He will reign on David's throne and over his kingdom, establishing and upholding it with justice and righteousness from that time on and forever. The zeal of the LORD Almighty will accomplish this.

—ISAIAH 9:6–7

In this verse Isaiah expresses the heart of God when he says there will be no end to the greatness of His government and peace. The Lord often reminds me of this passage and how there is no end in the kingdom of God. If we believe that God's gifts and His call are irrevocable, then we must see that there will be no end for those who follow Him. Understanding that there is no end is what allows us to walk in victory!

Chapter 5

COVENANT AND **TESTING**

As we go through life, we will be blessed with various types of relationships. Some will be simple friendships, conducted in passing, while others will take on more prominent roles in our future. Understanding the importance of covenant relationships is paramount if we are going to walk in everything God has for us.

As discussed in the first chapter, our journey with the Lord begins on the day we accept Jesus as our Savior and the light of our life. Our spiritual walk with Him is a relationship based in covenant, just as marriage is a covenant relationship! As with any covenant relationship, we can expect to go through periods of testing with the Lord that will ultimately strengthen our testimony and build our faith. Our salvation comes by the hand of God and is established in covenant by His love, grace, and promises.

Those who enter a covenant relationship must be willing to honor the commitments associated with that relationship. When God called us out of the old covenant and into the new, He changed the requirements that had bound us to condemnation under the law.

> For God so loved the world that he gave his one and only
> Son, that whoever believes in him shall not perish but have
> eternal life.
>
> —John 3:16

God gave His only Son as a sacrifice for our sins and in doing so made a covenant of salvation with all who believe. John 15:13 says, "Greater love has no one than this: to lay down one's life for one's friends." As we move through life, relationships based in love and grace will stand the test of time. In marriage, for example, legalism and condemnation do not provide a good foundation for a loving, covenant relationship. On the other hand, a willingness to sacrifice your own life and desires does.

Romans chapter 3 tells us that all have sinned and fallen short of the glory of God. If we go through life with an understanding that love and grace are the foundation, and apply it to our own relationships, God will restore His glory in covenant. When God set the boundaries of covenant with His people, He asked that they do one thing, and that was to remain faithful to Him. God even referred to Himself as a bridegroom and His people the bride. Our own wedding vows mirror God's call to salvation in their covenant requirements to forsake all others and commit to each other in sickness and health, for better or worse, and in good times and bad. These values that allow us to better understand covenant relationship in marriage also detail some of the tests we may face in learning to walk together as one flesh. In the same way, God designed us to become one with His Spirit and called us to remain in Him as He remains in us. Inside the boundaries of covenant God has created a place for us to triumph over hardship as He builds our character until we reach maturity.

I have often thought about how long it takes to build trust in a relationship. Can trust be established in a moment, or does it take time for trust to mature and become faith? God's Word reminds us often of His record of faithfulness in times of trouble and encourages us to take joy in our own suffering because it produces maturity and hope. Even when we go through times of suffering, God can use our circumstances to strengthen our faith.

As we grow in our walk with the Lord over time, it allows us to look back at our past and see how He has shown Himself faithful to us again and again. In this way, our relationship with God deepens, and trust matures into an unwavering faith in His character and dedication to war for us in times of trouble.

WHO IS CALLED TO WAR?

God will place many people and relationships in your life. The time will come, however, when you'll have to determine who is called to fight beside you in the midst of warfare. In this process God will show you which relationships will stand the test of time and those that can be bent or broken under stress. Someone once said, "There are friends you go to war with, and then there are friends you go to lunch with." The Holy Spirit will show you which ones.

In some situations warfare doesn't seem logical, but when God calls on us to fight, we need to be willing to act on His voice. Many in His kingdom have been given a DNA for warfare in worship and intercession. He calls out that gift inside them to take ground from the enemy and establish His kingdom. Just as God showed Gideon which soldiers to take into battle, He will also show those who carry the DNA for warfare His plan for victory. "For the Lord GOD does nothing without revealing his secret to his servants the prophets" (Amos 3:7, ESV). How much more will the Lord reveal to us today who carry His Spirit within us? "Now we have received, not the spirit of the world, but the Spirit who is from God," penned Paul, "that we might know the things that have been freely given to us by God" (1 Cor. 2:12, NKJV). One of these things that we have been given is our battle plan.

God had to take those who did not have an awareness for battle and remove them from Gideon's ranks. He did this so

Israel would not boast of their own power but acknowledge that their victory belonged to the Lord. In the end God used those with an understanding of His purposes to drive the enemy's camp into confusion.

Warfare not only breaks us through personally but also moves the kingdom of God into new ground corporately. We must wage war against the enemy of our souls to see personal breakthrough in areas where Satan and the powers of darkness have kept us bound up. On a corporate level we serve a kingdom that will not pass away, and it is our desire to see it extend to every corner of the earth. To have a kingdom mindset means understanding that the kingdom advances through warfare. In our covenant walk with the Lord, He will call on us to discern times and seasons and to know when to war against principalities and powers that do not represent His kingdom.

COVENANT FOUNDATIONS

One day as I was praying, the Lord asked me, "How does covenant apply right now when the world all around you is shaking?" This was during the coronavirus pandemic of 2020. Nations were being shaken. Economies and world structures began to collapse or change strategies in an attempt to survive.

In the midst of all this chaos, God began to move and restore the foundations of covenant in His house. I watched as many ministries and believers from nations all over the world pulled together to establish a voice in the eye of this storm that was blowing in every direction.

During that time, God reminded me of a dream I had experienced a few months before the pandemic. In the dream I was standing in a lion's cage like you would find in a modern zoo. I was washing the windows and rearranging the enclosure in the belief that the cage was empty. Suddenly I could feel a presence behind me. When I turned around, I found myself face to face with the fiercest lion I'd ever seen, staring directly into my eyes. My heart almost stopped, and I froze. Strangely, the lion silently watched me as I went about cleaning the enclosure. I realized that he had been watching me the whole time. As I sought the Lord for the meaning of that dream, He spoke to me and said that He was preparing to clean and rearrange His house, and that wherever man thought things were under his own power, God would be watching over him.

In the next few months after that we watched God rearrange our ministry in Jerusalem in ways that we could not have imagined. The ministry had been operating for three years with a growing local congregation. Things were running smoothly from week to week without many of the pressures we had experienced in the beginning stages. Still, it seemed like something was missing. We began to believe that the expression God desired for us was not growing to reflect the full potential of what He had called us to establish.

In the early months of 2019 God spoke to me very clearly and said that He would reestablish the Glory of Zion Ministry Center in Jerusalem on a new model and allow various expressions of His Spirit to come full circle. I came into agreement with what the Lord had spoken without an understanding of how He would bring it to pass. This is how the Holy Spirit often works in our lives. He gives us the vision and then just enough information to take the next step forward in faith. God wants us to trust Him as He illuminates the path before us. Remember, as we said in chapter 1, "Since we live by the Spirit," Paul says, "let us keep in step with the Spirit" (Gal. 5:25). The Spirit of God leads us step by step as He unfolds the path before us.

In September of 2019 our ministry experienced a very tragic situation. This led to a challenging season when rumors and false accusations began to take a toll on the ministry. One by one, families that had been with us for years started to leave. It was extremely difficult to watch. Our weekly meetings continued to shrink until there was only a handful of people in the room for many of our services, sometimes fewer than ten. As I think about it now, I realize how many people simply didn't want to deal with any controversy in the body and would rather simply distance themselves than seek the truth. It's saddening to see how much division can occur when a spirit of accusation is allowed to take root.

As we endured this intense season, God began to show us those who were called to go to war with us. We could see clearly that some relationships would be established through testing, while others would fade into the background. Some we thought were close friends decided to distance themselves and wait for the storm to end. This episode went on for several months and shook the entire ministry to the point of testing the very foundations that God had shown us to build on.

One morning Amber and I were discussing the direction of the ministry center and how we both felt this was the time God had set aside to restructure and renew. As the memory of what God had spoken to me earlier in the year came rushing back, I experienced a place of clarity in my ability to hear the Lord's voice like never before. Both Amber and I could clearly see the vision that God was speaking over the center and our staff.

The next day, we called our staff together and explained that we would be asking several of those whom God had placed with us to take positions of leadership in establishing a new expression the Lord was showing us. In the beginning it was difficult to communicate why we were making such drastic changes to the way the center had operated.

After several weeks went by, we watched in wonder as the Lord began to work in the gifts of those who were called to serve, while realigning the vision of the entire center. God used all these experiences to create a testimony in our lives and show us how seasons of testing could work to restore and strengthen the foundations of covenant.

Understanding that the foundation of our walk with the Lord is based on covenant allows us to see that even when the house around us is crumbling, God has a plan to rebuild in a new and stronger way. We watched God redefine the ministry center in

Jerusalem from a church model that we had been striving in for over three years to a kingdom model designed to serve covenant. God had to take us back and restore our understanding of His foundational design so that we could see the alignment He desired us to be in as we moved forward building our future. Unless the foundation was built on covenant, the structure would not reflect the kingdom of God or serve His wider purposes in the earth. In Ephesians chapter 2 we can see His order in covenant set forth. The Holy Spirit burned this passage into my spirit.

> [Build] on the foundation of the apostles and prophets, with Christ Jesus himself as the chief cornerstone. In him the whole building is joined together and rises to become a holy temple in the Lord. And in him you too are being built together to become a dwelling in which God lives by his Spirit.
>
> —EPHESIANS 2:20–22

As a body we have to allow God to build us up in covenant according to His design as one new man, whether Jew or Gentile. As God draws us closer to Himself, He will bring us into a holy place set apart for His Spirit to come alive and dwell inside His people.

ALIGNING WITH COVENANT

As I was praying about covenant, God showed me a picture of a well-oiled machine.

For a machine to function properly, it has to be well oiled and each part must be properly aligned. A machine that is not lubricated properly can get out of alignment and will not produce at full capacity or will produce a flawed product. It's important for us to grasp that God is trying to align every part of His body in such a way as to produce forward movement in His kingdom. His desire is to see every gift of His Spirit operating at the full capacity He designed it for. When we yield gifts to God and allow Him to bring them into proper alignment, under the oil of His anointing, it allows us to become what He has destined for us.

Building on the foundation of apostles and prophets realigns us with covenant design and opens the doors for God's Spirit to move. This is the DNA and building blocks to realigning the Lord's house in covenant. When the Holy Spirit moves freely through these gifts, the rest of His house will have a foundation to build on that is led by the Spirit of God.

> So Christ himself gave the apostles, the prophets, the evangelists, the pastors and teachers, to equip his people for works of service, so that the body of Christ may be built up until we all reach unity in the faith and in the knowledge of the Son of God and become mature, attaining to the whole measure of the fullness of Christ.
> —Ephesians 4:11–13

In today's world the apostolic and prophetic gifts are often misunderstood. A while back I attended a meeting of leaders in Israel. At one point in the meeting I looked directly at one of the leaders and acknowledged that he had an apostolic anointing at work in his life. One of the other attendants immediately confronted me and said that in the past she had been severely hurt by an apostolic ministry. As a result she no longer trusted anyone who called himself or herself an apostle. The leader that I had spoken the affirming word to then turned to me and asked that I not use the word *apostle* because many in the room had similar sentiments. He further commented that he did not believe labels were necessary.

This conversation has repeated itself in similar ways with other leaders over the years who did not believe that the apostolic and prophetic gifts are still operational in today's church as they were in biblical times. Some of these people have even gone so far as to level personal attacks against me over who my father is and his teachings concerning the apostolic and prophetic gifts.

It surprises me whenever I meet someone who believes in the

gift of prophecy but discounts the apostolic. I have met several who have a prophetic gifting but operate outside any form of accountability. It has been my observation that someone with a strong prophetic gift can cast vision for God's people when fully submitted to the Lord. When the gift of prophecy is not properly submitted to the Spirit of God, the devil can gain access and use that same gift of spiritual sight to speak into that person in a way that is not from God. The spiritual gift of prophecy can cross over into witchcraft when used to serve man's interest instead of the Spirit of God.

In 1 Corinthians 14 the apostle Paul instructed his followers to eagerly desire the gifts of the Spirit, especially that of prophecy, as the prophetic gift serves to edify, encourage, and build up the church. Again we can see that the gift of prophecy is referred to as instrumental in building up the body, just as Ephesians said that prophecy would be the foundation along with the apostolic. Although God's Word says to test the word of the prophets, we must understand that He gave us the gift of spiritual sight, and we need it to establish our foundation on a vision that He has set forth. The apostle Paul gained an understanding of this on the road to Damascus. In Acts chapter 9 we see that Saul (later called Paul) was traveling to Damascus to continue in his persecution of believers. The religious and legalistic structure in Jerusalem would stop at nothing in their attempt to destroy the move of God's Spirit that was taking place in the nations.

As Paul neared the city of Damascus, the bright and penetrating light of God suddenly flashed around him. It was so intense that it knocked Paul to the ground and blinded him. Then Jesus spoke out of the light. After pondering this account many times, I do not think it was a coincidence that God used blindness to get Paul's attention. Paul had to be blinded in the natural so that he could see in the spiritual. God was also revealing something to Paul about the prophetic that he needed to understand in order to serve his call as an apostle and build on a foundation of covenant in the nations.

In verse 10 God began calling to a man named Ananias in a vision and told him to go visit Saul and restore his sight. Ananias initially argued that Saul was dangerous and had a reputation for persecuting Christians, yet God's only instruction to Ananias was to go!

> But the Lord said to Ananias, "Go! This man is my chosen instrument to proclaim my name to the Gentiles and their kings and to the people of Israel. I will show him how much he must suffer for my name."
>
> Then Ananias went to the house and entered it. Placing his hands on Saul, he said, "Brother Saul, the Lord—Jesus, who appeared to you on the road as you were coming here—has sent me so that you may see again and be filled with the Holy Spirit." Immediately, something like scales fell from Saul's eyes, and he could see again. He got up and was baptized, and after taking some food, he regained his strength.
>
> —Acts 9:15–19

Reading this passage has always impressed on me how critical the relationship between apostles and prophets is in order to become the foundation of the church. God's chosen instrument to proclaim His name to the nations needed the vision God sent to him through the prophet. Paul understood what it meant to be blind, but now he could see!

PART II:

PREPARING

FOR WHAT'S

AHEAD

Chapter 6

STRENGTH IN **DARKNESS**

WHEN AN ATMOSPHERE of sin is cultivated, it brings a person or nation into darkness and separation from God. Many of us have experienced this personally at some point and have had to let God deliver us from sin issues in our own lives. Our walk with the Lord requires us to continue on a path of repentance and let the light of God invade every dark corner of our lives.

You know that nagging feeling you get when something just isn't right and you start to lose vision and hope for the future? Depression and a state of spiritual death are the inevitable result when sin is allowed to take root in your life. In the natural we tend to think of death from a physical standpoint without realizing how we can become dead to the voice of God. When God first breathed life into us, He set us in motion, and our lives are linked with His movement. God's Word says that He knit us together in our mothers' wombs and knew us before we were born (Ps. 139). Our strength when we are surrounded by darkness is linked to our faith in God's design and purpose. Our ability to move forward in that purpose becomes the driving force in our lives. Finding our purpose, according to the design for which we were created, brings us into personal peace that strengthens our understanding of who God is.

As you read through the Word, you can see the effect that sin has to separate us from our source of life. As soon as you take your eyes off life, you begin to come into agreement with death. We have to allow God's light to push back every area of darkness in us so we can come into communion with His light. I love this passage from 1 John that speaks about God being the light that pushes back all darkness.

> This is the message we have heard from him and proclaimed to you, that God is light, and in him there is no darkness at all. If we say we have fellowship with him while we walk in darkness, we lie and do not practice the truth. But if we walk in the light, as he is in the light, we have fellowship with one another, and the blood of Jesus his Son cleanses us from all sin.
>
> —1 JOHN 1:5–7, ESV

When I was growing up, I took art classes from a man who lived down the street. One day I asked him why he had chosen to become a professional artist and what motivated him to continue his work. His simple yet profound response never left me: "I fell in love with the light."

In later years I would ponder this statement in reference to my own walk with the Lord, as God revealed to me how we must fall in love with His light. After God separated the heavens from the earth in Genesis, He spoke and said, "Let there be light." In that very moment, the power of His voice began to create. We have to understand God as a creator to fall in love with His light. When we stop and remember that God is the author of all creation, the light, which is a reflection of His presence, can penetrate our atmosphere.

> For in him all things were created: things in heaven and on earth, visible and invisible, whether thrones or powers or rulers or authorities; all things have been created through

him and for him. He is before all things, and in him all
things hold together.

—COLOSSIANS 1:16–17

Seeing that God has the ability to create light in every area of
our lives brings us into faith that His light will be our strength,
and He can decree light even in our darkest moments.

SEPARATING SIN FROM SINNERS— THE POWER OF LOVE

In my life and relationship with the Lord, I have grown in my
understanding of God's love for us, and I continue to seek His
heart for the restoration of righteousness. As you read through
the Word of God, you can see that Jesus surrounded Himself not
with those who were considered righteous but with those who
were in need of His grace. In Luke, when Jesus had eaten dinner
with a tax collector named Levi, the Pharisees came to Him in a
spirit of judgment to question why He would keep company with
sinners and tax collectors.

> Jesus answered them, "It is not the healthy who need a
> doctor, but the sick. I have not come to call the righteous,
> but sinners to repentance."
>
> —LUKE 5:31–32

Understanding repentance and grace is key to separating sin
from sinners. We must learn to operate in the same love that the
Father has to see people separately from their sins. As believers we
must learn to walk in repentance. Both Jesus and John the Baptist
came preaching a message of repentance because the kingdom of
heaven draws near.

> In those days John the Baptist came, preaching in the wil-
> derness of Judea and saying, "Repent, for the kingdom
> of heaven has come near." This is he who was spoken of
> through the prophet Isaiah: "A voice of one calling in the

wilderness, 'Prepare the way for the Lord, make straight paths for him.'"

—MATTHEW 3:1–3

In verse 8 John goes on to rebuke the Pharisees and Sadducees and tell them to produce fruit in keeping with repentance. We repent of our sins at the very moment of our salvation, but we must continue to walk in repentance. Matthew chapter 3 speaks of two baptisms—the baptism of water for repentance, and a baptism of fire that Jesus would bring in His power.

> I baptize you with water for repentance. But after me comes one who is more powerful than I, whose sandals I am not worthy to carry. He will baptize you with the Holy Spirit and fire. His winnowing fork is in his hand, and he will clear his threshing floor, gathering his wheat into the barn and burning up the chaff with unquenchable fire.
>
> —MATTHEW 3:11–12

When we are baptized with the Holy Spirit, all of a sudden an unquenchable fire begins to burn inside us, and we are able to hear the voice of God. When God's voice comes in power, it separates the harvest from all impurities, all sins, and all issues of the heart that stand between us and experiencing the kingdom of heaven. The Spirit of God will separate the chaff in your life and remove it from the threshing floor. We enter in through repentance, and then God sets the fire that pushes back darkness.

> For the word of God is alive and active. Sharper than any double-edged sword, it penetrates even to dividing soul and spirit, joints and marrow; it judges the thoughts and attitudes of the heart. Nothing in all creation is hidden from God's sight. Everything is uncovered and laid bare before the eyes of him to whom we must give account.
>
> —HEBREWS 4:12–13

Holding on to our sinful nature and flesh patterns causes us to live in a state of darkness. When we are filled with the Holy Spirit, the spoken word of God comes alive and begins to separate us from our sinful nature as a double-edged sword divides bone from marrow. In my own life the Lord continues to show me areas of darkness that have held me back from experiencing the kingdom of heaven. This is why it is so important for us to walk in repentance as we read in 1 John. God's kingdom is all around us, and we need His light shining the way.

BIBLICAL RESTORATION

Years ago my father was dealing with several individuals in his ministry who had fallen into sin in their personal lives. At the time, I had only been serving in full-time ministry for a short period and struggled with how the situation was being handled. I went to my father and confronted him, asking what would become of us if it became public that some of those serving the ministry had fallen into such gross sin. After a long argument my father angrily declared that his ministry was one based on grace, and if I could not agree with that, I needed to ask the Lord to show me where I was called. I pondered this discussion for several days before deciding to give my concerns to the Lord and continue serving the ministry in the capacity He had placed me in. For the next several years I watched as God did a tremendous work in the lives of those who had fallen. The end result was that marriages were reconciled and healing replaced the brokenness of infidelity.

In that season, God did a powerful work in my heart as I witnessed the power of His grace in the darkest moments of someone's life. After having my own revelation of grace, I went back to my dad and repented for my attitude of judgment in years past. I then asked him to share with me how he saw grace.

Dad began to share testimony after testimony of times he had seen people restored because God was given the freedom to work in them when they hit rock bottom. He went on to explain how we can all receive the grace of God over our sins, but we must develop a relationship with the Holy Spirit to walk in His favor and be guided by His grace. Amber will share her experience with grace in the next chapter.

People often are not able to step into a true relationship with the Holy Spirit until they are forced to deal with the issues of their hearts. When someone goes through a traumatic event such as infidelity, it can be extremely difficult for the family and others who have been wounded to get past it. Yet many are restored to a true relationship with the Holy Spirit and a richness with the Lord that they might have never experienced.

To this day I continue to be a student of God's grace and His continuous working in our lives to restore the condition of our hearts. As a leader in ministry I make it a priority to seek direction from the Holy Spirit on how we can apply grace within the body of Christ. We need God's light ever shining to draw out of darkness those He has us walking with.

We live in a day and age in which Christian leaders falling into gross sin has become all too common. The exposure of such events has done significant damage to the community of faith, destroying ministries and leading many individuals to question their own faith. Now understand, I personally believe there is an appropriate time for sin to be exposed and dealt with! As leaders we have a high responsibility to those who place their trust in us. When a situation exists that presents a clear violation of the law or moral conduct according to biblical standards, it forces us to evaluate what information must be released and what actions will best serve the ones who've placed their trust in those leaders.

Unfortunately leaders are flawed humans that make mistakes too. I do believe that making a mistake that has to be taken to the Lord for restoration is different from willfully choosing to continue in gross sin without repentance. The latter should preclude someone from leadership in ministry.

The focus and the standard in such cases should be true repentance!

This being said, how we handle these situations within the community of leaders has a direct effect on public perception of the Christian body. Faith in ministries as a whole will be affected much more by decisions made in times of crisis. As leaders it is incumbent upon us to seek the Lord's wisdom when we are called on to manage such situations.

Sometimes the good faith placed in us by those who follow our ministries may not be best served by our own engagement in social media wars. Sometimes the manner in which public statements are made can become more destructive than constructive. If we are not sensitive to the Holy Spirit in the way we communicate, our actions may have far-reaching negative effects and lead to many unanticipated consequences. The event of whistleblowing in the age of social media allows almost anyone to say whatever they want publicly. As more and more individuals take to the internet in attempts to expose a variety of grievances, we need to be discerning and consider the source.

Recently someone made public statements about me and our ministry. This individual simply didn't agree with some decisions that were made and took it upon himself to try and destroy the ministry and discredit my work as a minister. He also made a statement that he would expose all the ministries in the area and destroy them as well. Some of the very public accusations that were made include that we were running a cult, mistreating our employees, and mismanaging the ministry's finances. All these accusations were wholly untrue, and a matter of record with both our accountants and the court system. The public nature of these accusations caused many, including other leaders, to question the ministry and my integrity, regardless of the fact that the individual making these statements had no firsthand knowledge of my life or the inner workings of the ministry center.

I shared my personal experience before delving deeper into the discussion because it illustrates how much personal damage an accusation can cause in the absence of facts, evidence, and spiritual discernment. All three—facts, evidence, and discernment—are needed before we even consider morality, legalities, and simple wisdom. There is a spirit of accusation at work in the earth that operates in lies, assumptions, and half-truths. It's an attempt to destroy the body of Christ and the work of those who serve the Lord.

As leaders moving in covenant, we are responsible to God for what comes out of our mouths! It brings to mind a particular passage in Matthew 15:11, where Jesus said that it is not what goes into a man's mouth but what comes out that makes him unclean. Verses 18–20 go on to say that the mouth is a reflection of the heart, and the heart produces all forms of evil, including false testimony. It is a perfect illustration of how we can become so religious in our thinking that we fail to see the intentions of the heart. We must not forget that both sin and repentance take place in the heart.

With this understanding, I would suggest that we are also responsible for what we hear on many levels. While we may not be able to control what other people say, we can definitely control how we let the information we consume affect our own hearts. It has been my experience that people, including leaders, often take a one-sided story or a partial truth and fill in the blanks without ever contacting other parties involved. When this happens, it can allow the devil a foothold of accusation seeded by false testimony. When we allow false testimony to settle into our hearts and become our version of truth, it becomes a sin that we must repent of.

About four months after the accusation against our ministry, a young woman whom we have known for several years called my wife and said she felt that she needed to repent for blindly believing some things she'd heard without coming to us about it first. This young lady's willingness to obey the Holy Spirit's prompting to call us and share blessed us beyond description. It also was a step forward in our healing. I felt that justice was being restored and began to thank the Lord for His revelation that breaks the power of accusation. It reminds me of Revelation chapter 12, where a loud voice in heaven can be heard decreeing that he who has been accusing the brothers and sisters before God will be cast down!

> Now have come the salvation and the power and the kingdom of our God, and the authority of his Messiah. For the accuser of our brothers and sisters, who accuses them before God day and night, has been hurled down.
> —REVELATION 12:10

The above scripture says, "Now have come the salvation and the power and the kingdom of our God, and the authority of his Messiah." Taking this to heart, I am also reminded that Jesus continually said that God's kingdom draws near to us. In Psalm 89 we can hear the passion for the restoration of His kingdom in the earth and the establishment of His throne.

> Your arm is endowed with power; your hand is strong, your right hand exalted. Righteousness and justice are the foundation of your throne; love and faithfulness go before you. Blessed are those who have learned to acclaim you, who walk in the light of your presence, LORD. They rejoice in your name all day long; they celebrate your righteousness. For you are their glory and strength, and by your favor you exalt our horn. Indeed, our shield belongs to the LORD, our king to the Holy One of Israel.
> —PSALM 89:13–18

When God raises His hand against the accuser, righteousness and justice are restored, and His kingdom will begin to manifest in the earth as it is in heaven. Walking in the light of His presence pushes back darkness and becomes our strength. As we rejoice in His name, He restores our joy, and we celebrate His righteousness. Our shield belongs to Him, and our covering and shelter are by the grace of His salvation.

Revelation 12 goes on to say that we overcome by the blood of the Lamb and the power of our testimony. This is why we see God act with power to establish a testimony in people's transgressions.

Great grace leads us to a strong testimony, and our testimony becomes a weapon that we use to overcome under the power of His blood. When we can say, "But God did this in my life," it renders the enemy powerless to accuse us any longer and establishes the purity of God's truth in justice and righteousness.

When we see that God has established His throne as a foundation of justice and righteousness, we begin to understand how grace covers us under the spirit of the law when the letter of the law destroys in its conviction. God uses both conviction and grace to bring us to true repentance in our restoration. When we begin to walk in repentance, God will draw us into an experience with His kingdom through the baptism of His Holy Spirit and grace. When grace becomes our testimony, we overcome the accuser, and the Spirit of God cuts off darkness and covers us under His sacrifice. There's a growing desperation in my generation for a standard of righteousness to be restored. As we hunger and thirst for righteousness, God's Word promises we will be filled!

TESTIMONY IN DARK PLACES

In His grace God has allowed me to witness and experience various forms of darkness. Walking through dark places and situations both sharpens our discernment and builds our faith in His ability to surround us. We can trust God's hedge of protection and that He will act on our behalf to further His kingdom in the earth. The gates of hell will not stand against Him!

Over the years, Amber and I have been blessed to travel and serve the Lord in many different nations where the spiritual darkness is heavy. One particular trip jumps to mind. We had been to India once before, but our second trip would become one of the most powerful testimonies of God's power at work in dark places that I have ever witnessed.

We landed in New Dehli and boarded a second flight to Bagdogra Airport in the West Bengal district of northern India. The airport is used by the Indian military for fighter patrols and allows only a small number of civilian flights to land daily. I looked out the window next to my seat as a long line of fighter jets lined up next to us, each waiting its turn to take off.

Our driver met us outside the airport, and we began the three-hour drive farther east to the hotel where we would be staying for the next eight days. The scenery was some of the most beautiful I have ever experienced. Living in Israel, we have become accustomed to the dry climate and deserts that encompass most of West Asia. I didn't know how much I missed green until we drove through the lush patches of jungle interrupted by tea plantations in eastern India. Yet just underneath the surface of all the natural beauty lay a deep-rooted spiritual darkness—a state of bondage and demonic oppression on the people of that region that had transcended many generations. Soon I, too, would experience that dark oppression.

We arrived at the hotel late that night, and our team leader from England asked the hotel manager whether it was still possible to get something to eat before bed. As we entered the dining hall, prominently displayed was a shrine that stood along one of the walls. A closer look revealed that this structure served as a dwelling place for a pale-blue idol with numerous arms who sat ominously facing the room.

Over the next several days, I noticed the hotel manager and staff would take regular breaks from their routines to stand in front of this idol to commune with and pray to it. I asked the hotel manager what this ritual represented to him and what he believed. With a smile, he nodded his head to one side and began to explain that in Hindu culture, families and territories would be dedicated to a patron deity and show respect so that good luck and protection would follow.

As the conversation continued, I began to pray for this man and his family to be free from the oppression that was so tangible in the air. I sensed a state of confusion associated with the spiritism surrounding this idol and a heaviness that rested over the hotel and its staff. Throughout the rest of our trip almost every shop, restaurant, or other public place we entered had one of these shrines with an associated idol that represented a demonic spirit to which the property and its inhabitants had been dedicated.

Almost everyone we met in India had a good disposition and treated us kindly. As we entered into intercession leading up to the day of our meetings, God began to break our hearts for the people. We watched as a group of workmen constructed a large stage and set up a kitchen tent with little more than bamboo. Another team went to work advertising the event by simply driving through local villages with a bullhorn announcing the festival. Leaders in charge of the event managed to get permission from the government to host a Christian festival in a large field just outside town. We knew God was moving on our behalf because it was a miracle that these meetings were even approved. Most government officials in the area came from devout Hindu families and frowned on allowing such events. Clearly the hand of God was moving in the midst of the people. A hunger and thirst for righteousness stood in stark contrast to the spiritual darkness that had dominated the land for many generations.

Eight thousand people filled the field on the first morning! Family by family they came walking from surrounding villages and townships until there was hardly room to stand. From the start the crowd erupted into dance and praise as local worship teams played their music in Hindi. A feeling of joy swept the atmosphere, and the presence of God fell as we worshipped.

After the music ended, local pastors took the stage and shared testimonies of Jesus' power to restore lives, heal the sick, and cast out demons. After several such testimonies, they called for those who were sick, injured, or suffering from oppression to come forward for prayer. The effects of the spiritual darkness and demonic oppression became evident as hundreds of people rushed up for prayer.

Amber and I began to minister to the people one by one. They had every type of ailment you could imagine, from minor aches and pains, to cancer and kidney failure, to depression and addictions. Most simply wanted a touch from the supernatural God. There's nothing quite as fulfilling as seeing captives set free from bondages and wounded souls restored by God's power. It has always been a driving desire of mine to witness supernatural signs and wonders firsthand, just as Jesus said we would. But more than that, it's a desire to see people fall in love with the Light of the Lord, and for that Light to overtake their darkness.

In India we witnessed one person after another receive healing. One woman had a large cyst growing from her neck to the point that she could not hold her head upright. Amber began to decree her healing, and right before our eyes the lump shrank until it was completely gone. Another woman was dying from kidney failure and was bleeding from her mouth when her relatives asked us to come and pray for her. Several days later we found out that she received her healing. Others who had come on crutches and in wheelchairs walked away with a new understanding of who God is and the love He has for them.

Though in the past I've experienced personal healing and have seen others healed on multiple occasions, what we witnessed during those few days in India was unlike anything I had ever seen before. God was building my faith on a foundation of understanding the power of His kingdom even in the darkest of places.

On the last evening of meetings, our good friend Trevor Baker of Revival Fires Ministries stood up and began to speak about salvation and how a relationship with Jesus could bring deliverance from the bondage of generational curses and the spiritual darkness of demonic oppression. When the call to salvation came, three thousand people stood and gave their lives to Jesus. This event showed that God is strong even in our weakness, and His kingdom is in our midst. Our strength can be found in His name no matter what kind of darkness might surround us.

STRENGTH IN KNOWING

There is a verse in Luke chapter 13 where Jesus was in Jerusalem performing miracles and the Pharisees came to warn Him that

Herod was planning to kill Him if He did not leave the city. Jesus rebuked them and said, "Go tell that fox I must go on."

> At that time some Pharisees came to Jesus and said to him, "Leave this place and go somewhere else. Herod wants to kill you." He replied, "Go tell that fox, 'I will keep on driving out demons and healing people today and tomorrow, and on the third day I will reach my goal.' In any case, I must press on today and tomorrow and the next day—for surely no prophet can die outside Jerusalem!"
>
> —Luke 13:31–33

This passage inspires me to consider those things God must do to fulfill prophecy and affect the move of His kingdom in the earth. Jesus never let the fear of man, or the law, distract Him from His mission. Rather, His face was set like flint on pleasing His heavenly Father and accomplishing the assignment He'd been given. Jesus moved in signs, wonders, and miracles and said that He "must press on," even when confronted with the threat of death.

Likewise, we have to move past the threat of death to understand that God has a set time when He will rebuke legalism to establish His kingdom. God can break the law of death when our lives are submitted to Him. As we walk out from under the shadow of death, fear is unable to affect the faith we have in our own testimony to overcome.

Revelation chapter 12 speaks of victory over Satan in the heavens and the establishment of the kingdom of God. It says that those who did not love their lives so much as to shrink from death triumphed over Satan by the blood of the Lamb and the word of their testimony (v. 11). The heavens and those who dwell in them are instructed to rejoice when the devil is cast down from heavenly places.

We can access the power of heaven and defeat death when we give the love of our own lives to the Lord. The joy of the Lord becomes our strength in dark places, and it comes from the victory that we know lies before us. Jesus Himself was our example in this. He endured the suffering of the cross and experienced victory because He could see what lay before Him. "For the joy set before him he endured the cross, scorning its shame, and sat down at the right hand of the throne of God" (Heb. 12:2). Jesus did not love His life as to shrink from death.

We have strength in knowing that God will pass through any dark area in our lives and that no matter how the atmosphere around us has been affected, the gates of hell will not overcome the kingdom of God!

Chapter 7

WARRING AGAINST
INVISIBLE **ENEMIES**

WHEN I (DANIEL) was a kid, my father and I would watch TV shows together. This was how I spent quality time with him after all my younger siblings went to bed. My bedtime was later than theirs, so I would look forward to those last couple of hours watching shows like *I Love Lucy*, *Little House on the Prairie*, or one of the westerns that came on regular programming every night.

One of those nights in particular had a lifelong impact on me. I was seven years old, and as usual, we were watching *Little House on the Prairie*. The show began with a dark and ominous feeling that was not characteristic of most episodes. The opening scene took place at night, with two men tending to their sheep as an eerie fog surrounded them. One of the men was examining the sheep and found that the animal was infected with anthrax. Instead of taking measures to prevent further contamination, the two men decided to butcher the sheep and sell the meat. This led to an outbreak of anthrax that killed many families that lived on surrounding farms.

My dad watched as I sat glued to the TV screen with a look of fear on my face. Before viewing that episode, I had no reference point for someone purposefully making others sick or the idea of a deadly disease causing an epidemic. Because much of my early childhood was spent in poor health, the idea of sickness was something I was already fearful of. On that night, though, my fear reached a whole new level as my young mind processed what was playing out on the screen.

Over the next several days I began obsessively asking my parents questions about anthrax in the hope that their answers would bring me some kind of peace. After answering the best they could, my parents became a bit concerned. The two of them sat me down and asked why I had so many questions about anthrax. Why was I so scared? We had a long discussion, and then they prayed for me.

After they finished praying, I remember my dad looking at me and asking, "So, Daniel, what have you been asking God for?"

"To catch a butterfly," I replied. "But I never can. They keep flying away."

The next morning, my dad and I were standing in the front yard when this beautiful butterfly just landed on my shoulder. That had never happened before, and I knew it was from God. I gently cupped my hand over the butterfly, looked up to the sky, and told God that I could see how much He loved me. I lifted my hand to let the butterfly go, and an interesting thing happened. The butterfly sat on my shoulder for just a moment and then flapped his wings and flew away. As the butterfly flew away, so did my fear, and I never struggled with it again. However, the Lord spoke to my dad in his quiet time and said that although I had been delivered from a spirit of fear, anthrax would indeed visit America when I was twenty years old.

Over the years, I continued to learn about the white powder, as I love to read and research anything that has to do with history or science. My grandfather on my dad's side, Alfred Croix, was an excellent source of information. A Texas A&M graduate, he served as the Denton County agricultural agent for many years. I grew up working cattle out in the fields with Grandpa Croix, and he taught me most of what I know about zoonotic diseases and the care of livestock. Anthrax in its natural form is caused by a bacteria called *Bacillus anthracis*, which originates in soil and can be transmitted to humans through contact with infected livestock. It has also been widely researched for its viability as a biological weapon. Many countries with bioweapons programs have cultured and stockpiled large quantities of anthrax for deterrence and potential use on the battlefield.

Anthrax made headlines in the United States in 2001 after letters laced with spores from the substance were mailed to locations in Florida, New York, New Jersey, Connecticut, and Washington, DC. This act of bioterrorism killed five people and sickened seventeen more.[1] After the attack the United States was left with a new reality that required increased security measures that would change how we prepare for the threat of bioterrorism in the future.

Just as the Lord had spoken to my dad thirteen years earlier, the United States was faced with anthrax on my twentieth birthday. The first case was diagnosed on October 4, and I turned twenty years old on October 7, 2001. When all this happened, I had just started working for the Denton County Sheriff's Office. It had only been a month since the terrorist attacks of 9/11, and the entire country was still in a state of shock. Being faced with biological terrorism from an apparent domestic source was enough to spark fear in most people. Most of us were a little more careful when checking our mail.

One day I was driving by the post office in Denton and saw an ambulance and fire truck parked outside, with several firemen suiting up to go inside. A package leaking white powder had been discovered. As a result the entire building had to be shut down while the parcel was investigated for the possibility that it contained anthrax spores. This scenario played out in post offices all across the United States. Even though there were no signs of anthrax at most locations, the drain of energy and resources for emergency response and precautions to navigate through those circumstances was paralyzing. All of it was sparked by fear.

I HAVE NOT GIVEN YOU
A SPIRIT OF FEAR

> For God has not given us a spirit of fear, but of power and of
> love and of a sound mind.
> —2 Timothy 1:7, nkjv

As human beings, we all have something that triggers our deepest fears. God used the anthrax event in my life to show me that He knows what situations will trigger fear in us and how to best prepare for it. The Holy Spirit knows those weaknesses the enemy might exploit to destroy our faith or slow us down in our pursuit of what God has called us to do. Paul wrote in 2 Corinthians 2:11, "…that Satan might not outwit us. For we are not unaware of his schemes." Mark this down. Satan has schemes and attempts to outwit us. One of those schemes is fear.

The spirit of fear itself is an invisible enemy. When carefully considering most of the things that cause paralyzing fear in us, we soon realize it's the fear of the unknown that is at the root. When the devil has a foothold, he will use our own fear responses to create terror.

Our natural response to fear has to do with the way God designed us. There is healthy fear. Within God's grace we act to distance ourselves from danger or take actions that remove a potential threat. God designed us with the ability to hear His voice and discern situations that could push us out from under His covering.

I love this passage from Psalm 91. It reminds us that we dwell in the shelter of the Most High and rest in the shadow of the Almighty.

> Whoever dwells in the shelter of the Most High will rest in
> the shadow of the Almighty. I will say of the Lord, "He is
> my refuge and my fortress, my God, in whom I trust." Surely
> he will save you from the fowler's snare and from the deadly
> pestilence. He will cover you with his feathers, and under

his wings you will find refuge; his faithfulness will be your shield and rampart. You will not fear the terror of night, nor the arrow that flies by day, nor the pestilence that stalks in the darkness, nor the plague that destroys at midday.

—PSALM 91:1–6

The last verse says we will not fear the terror of night nor the pestilence that stalks in darkness. We must allow the Lord to take away our unhealthy fear of what exists in darkness. We take our shelter in the presence of the Most High, and the shadow that covers us is not one born of darkness but the shelter of His wings.

Reading over this passage, I'm reminded of the Passover story when the sons of Israel were instructed to take the blood of the sacrificial lamb and place it on the doorposts so that death would not visit their firstborn. As the Israelites were obedient in painting the entrances of their homes with blood, God faithfully marked their homes as shelters from the spirit of death that would come by night. Likewise, we have to ask the Lord where our abiding place is, and allow Him to cover us with the grace of His blood. When God speaks, accept the provisions of His shelter, and allow Him to mark out your boundaries as a refuge. Don't let Satan give you a spirit of fear when there is a provision for your covering.

As time went on, world events continued to test the faith God had given me over my fears of sudden disease outbreaks and the potential use of biochemical warfare. I remember watching the news in 1991 as US soldiers in Kuwait and Iraq suited up in full protective gear in anticipation that Saddam Hussein might deploy stockpiles of chemical weapons that he was believed to possess. Ironically those same weapons would pose an even more direct threat in my life many years later as they had been smuggled across the border into Syria. For several years after we moved to Israel in 2011, Syria's chemical weapons program was considered a grave threat to Israel.

The world has also seen several concerning disease outbreaks over the last couple of decades. Some of these events include the SARS epidemic of 2002, MERS in 2012, bubonic plague in

Madagascar in 2017, a sharp global increase in measles cases in 2019, the 2013–2016 Ebola virus outbreak that devastated West Africa, and now, COVID-19.

Although I kept up with most of these situations as they occurred, they did not pose an immediate threat to our family or cause us to drastically change our routines. Over the years, I had seen so many news reports of men dressed in space suits preparing to challenge the next weird tropical disease that I became accustomed to it. After the first SARS epidemic it became commonplace to see East Asians wearing paper medical masks, which seemed like an overreaction to me. Little did we know this would soon become our own new and rapidly changing reality.

In the last months of 2019 a strange new respiratory illness began to emerge in Hubei province, China. At first a small number of cases surfaced in Wuhan, a city with a population of eleven million. The new disease presented with flu-like symptoms, and rapidly progressed into respiratory distress in some patients. This type of illness was familiar to local doctors in the area due to the initial outbreak of SARS in 2002.

After several patients died from apparent cases of viral pneumonia, doctors began to sound the alarm in China. There were early reports of medical personnel and news reporters being threatened by the government and instructed not to spread rumors about the situation.

Reports that a small cluster of a novel coronavirus had been discovered in Wuhan began to spread through international media around the beginning of January 2020. World powers initially downplayed the situation as a localized problem while issuing travel advisories for China and other South Asian nations. As sparks thrown from a flame, new cases of COVID-19 began to appear in neighboring countries and predictably along air travel routes.

My wife, Amber, and I were preparing to travel to Wales to minister when news reports of the virus began to dominate the media. We had been looking forward to that trip for a long time and still felt that God had covered us to go. While in Wales, we connected with an apostolic center there and were blessed to retrace the steps of the Welsh Revival.

One day our host drove us out to visit the Bible College of Wales in Swansea, which was founded by Rees Howells in 1924. We walked the rooms in the reception area, reading about Mr. Howells' life and the intercession that took place during the Welsh Revival and World War II. After the tour ended, we had some time to visit with a young couple who were overseeing the college and managing groups of visitors and interns. I'll never forget the sigh of relaxation that came on their faces when we all sat down to share and pray. Amber and I soon learned they had been working around the clock to prepare for a group from Asia that would be arriving the following day. We watched their expressions of relaxation transform to ones of apprehension as they described the new precautions that were being taken due to the spread of coronavirus. A quarantine room had been set up for isolation should any of the new interns fall sick during their stay. After discussing prayer requests, the four of us spent some time in intercession for the protection of those at the Bible college and asking the Lord to give us His mind as to what He wants to accomplish during this trying season in the earth.

At the same time we were in Wales, three of our team members from Jerusalem had flown to France for a ski trip. As we all returned to Jerusalem, one of the team members started to feel ill. The other two showed up to our Sunday meeting. When we found out one of them had stayed home sick, I asked the other two to go home until their roommate's condition could be determined. Within twenty-four hours the news began to report that a cluster of coronavirus cases had been identified in France. After speaking to the doctor, our employee was considered low risk and asked not to go to the hospital. Another two days passed before the Israeli government released instructions for anyone traveling from France to self-quarantine for fourteen days from the date of entry. This meant that all three of our team members had to stay home for another week and a half.

I called our family doctor, who is also a close friend, and asked him what the situation was in Israel and whether we should follow any specific instructions at the ministry center. He reassured me that there were only fifteen cases in Israel and simply limiting meetings to fewer than a hundred persons was sufficient. We had planned a ministry trip to Thailand at the end of April and were concerned about the potential for our flights being canceled.

Shortly after that, the Israeli media began reporting cases in Thailand, and EL AL Airlines discontinued service to Bangkok from Israel. Flight after flight was canceled across Asia and some parts of Europe. The list of countries from which Israel mandated quarantine grew by the day. We went to the grocery store and stocked our freezer and pantry with a month's worth of supplies in anticipation of a possible government-mandated quarantine. It all still felt like a precaution, and we were optimistic that the COVID-19 epidemic would slowly fizzle out as spring approached.

Our world began to change on the night of March 6 when Amber received the call that her father, Jed Sauce, had passed away in Texas. The following day, our family had to make a split-second decision whether to try and travel to Texas to be with family or to stay in place at our home in Israel. Feeling at peace over our arrangements, we decided to board a flight immediately for Newark, New Jersey, and on to Dallas, Texas.

When we arrived in Dallas, it felt almost as if someone had hit the rewind button, as the United States was just starting to report small clusters of the virus in several states. It seemed that America was at the same point that Israel had been several weeks prior and would follow a similar pattern in transmission and its attempt to contain the spread of COVID-19. Within forty-eight hours we started the process all over again of stocking our home with enough food and supplies to last a long period of time should the government decide to take more drastic measures in the fight against this new enemy.

The director-general of the World Health Organization (WHO) labeled the spread of COVID-19 a pandemic. Further information stated that the number of active cases outside China had increased thirteenfold and affected 114 countries to date.[2] The WHO further noted that the word *pandemic* was not one to be used lightly, as it has the potential to cause a fear-based response in public perception that can be counterproductive to the fight against the spread of any disease. After detailing more numbers and statistics, the director-general stated that the WHO was ringing the alarm bell loud and clear.

From that point, things began moving at a rapid pace in the United States. President Donald Trump declared a national state of emergency in a press conference on Friday, March 13. A heavy, surreal reality dropped over me like a blanket as we watched the president and his team of advisers lay out the beginning stages of a plan addressing the developing situation. From the White House lawn the stage was set against a backdrop of beautiful cherry trees that were in full bloom. It just didn't seem to fit with the subject matter that was being discussed. First came reassurances that the federal government was working around the clock to make sure states and the medical community had access to test kits for the new virus. Many around the country were already concerned as patients were beginning to arrive at hospital emergency rooms and were unable to be tested in a timely manner.

It would also prove difficult to determine the true scope of the problem without the ability to quickly confirm cases. The president went on to discuss the possibility that localized quarantine orders could be issued in the coming days in an effort to slow the spike in transmission and allow hospitals to prepare for the coming influx of seriously ill patients.

The day after the state of emergency was declared, I went to the grocery store down the street from our home in Texas. As I walked the aisles, it became evident that our community had taken the president's announcement seriously. Many products that seemed abundant only days before were now noticeably absent from the shelves. Another shopper caught my attention as she stopped and gently pulled a cell phone out of her pocket to take pictures of the empty shelves. My stomach began to turn at the thought that the same social media outlets these pictures would likely be posted to might be our only social interaction in the days and weeks to come. Over the next couple of days the grocery stores became more depleted and began to ration some essential goods such as meat, milk, and paper products.

On a later trip to the store I stopped and spoke to one of the butchers who was placing meat on the shelves. Noticing that he looked worn out, I asked how he was doing in the midst of all these sudden changes. He took a few minutes to answer me and described how unsettling it had been for him to watch the way that fear had gripped the community. He had been on his feet for days restocking the meat section and could not move fast enough to keep food on the shelves. The atmosphere of fear had taken a toll on his emotions over time and worn him out both physically and mentally.

FACING MY FEAR

The first case of COVID-19 diagnosed in Denton County was reported on March 15. Dallas County, just to the south of Denton, had reported the first case only five days earlier, on March 10.

One night I went into the kitchen to pull some frozen chicken out of our freezer to thaw for the next day. It was around 11:30, I was tired, and this was the last thing I was planning to do before going to bed. I pulled the meat out and set it on the countertop just behind me. As I turned to shut the freezer door, I heard a glass fall on the island in the middle of our kitchen and begin to roll toward the edge. As a parent of small children, I'm used to catching falling objects before they hit the floor. Out of instinct I turned and grabbed for the glass to keep it from shattering on the kitchen floor. It bounced, and I managed to wrap my left hand around it just as it met the edge of our granite countertop. It was one of those large, thick glasses that we Texans like to drink iced tea from. I realized my mistake was serious the instant the glass shattered under my hand. And the immediate pain confirmed it. Covering my hand with a clean paper towel, which soaked with blood in seconds, I tried to wrap my head around what had just happened. When I pulled the paper away to look at the damage, it became apparent that I wasn't going to avoid a trip to the emergency room.

The spirit of fear wanted to rise up as my first thought was how the hospital was the last place I wanted to go in the middle of a disease epidemic. Sitting there in the kitchen, I envisioned the horror of walking into a crowded emergency room full of patients coughing and sneezing in the waiting area. As I was processing all this, Amber called my father, awakening him from a dead sleep, and asked whether he could take me to the emergency room because she needed to stay with our children. Dad arrived a few minutes later and walked into our kitchen, where we discussed our strategy for entering the emergency room. The anxiety on his face was clear.

After taking a breath and putting our heads together, we decided to go to a small 24-hour ER in our neighborhood with the hopes that it would be empty. Much to our dismay, it was shuttered and closed. This meant we would have to make the trip to Denton Regional Hospital, located a few minutes up the highway. Denton Regional is the largest medical complex in Denton County, and we both knew that anyone diagnosed with the virus would probably be receiving treatment there.

As we started toward the hospital, I asked Dad to call and see whether there were any special instructions for how we should enter. If you have ever seen Chuck Pierce speed down the highway while talking on a cell phone at night, that is a whole new kind of fear! After several attempts, Dad could not get a direct line to the hospital, so I took the phone and called 911. A Denton County dispatcher politely requested that we not break any traffic laws on the way to the hospital, and then she connected me with the emergency room.

Walking in the front door, we found a table set up where a nurse wearing protective gear was taking temperatures and asking questions about any possible exposure to the virus before patients could be admitted. I felt an air of relief as we walked into the waiting room and found it completely empty. God had allowed me to come to the hospital that night for a reason; He wanted me to remember that He was in complete control of all my fears. Peace washed over me as Dad and I walked down the hall and into the treatment room.

Over the next hour, four different nurses came in to wash my cut, take X rays, and prepare my hand for stitches. All of them were professional and comforting. Dad and I took a moment to pray for the staff who were treating me, for the protection of the hospital, and for the residents of Denton County as things would intensify with the virus. All the while the feeling of peace that God had given me strengthened, and a renewed sense of faith begin to arise inside me. Leaving the ER that night, it became clear that God had to bring me to the hospital to hear His voice, and what I heard would strengthen me in the battle to come.

As you go through your own life, remember that God will take you to a place where you can address your fears in order to strengthen you for your future. When God brings you to that place, there is nowhere safer. You can overcome your invisible enemy and rest in the shadow of His wings. Let your peace be restored and your faith arise! The peace that God gives us passes understanding. Beyond our own ability, we are able to supernaturally see and understand an enemy that was once invisible and unknown.

REVEALING YOUR ENEMY

Ever since this disease began to spread, the Holy Spirit has been revealing to me the parallels between spiritual warfare and the fight we experience in the natural. Just as a disease is an unseen enemy, our spiritual fight is one waged against powers and principalities of the air. As God showed me this, I began to pray that this enemy disease would be exposed and the authority it has in the air would be brought out of the darkness and into the light.

On Wednesday, March 18, President Trump made a statement that the fight against COVID-19 in the United States would now be classified under wartime provisions that allow the government to work with private companies to produce much-needed medical supplies. He also referred to the fight we are in as an all-out war being waged against an invisible enemy. Further statements made it clear that the government did not expect this fight to be easy.

Over the next several weeks we watched as one community after another imposed mandatory quarantine orders. Many other restrictions would come down the pike as the government tried to manage the number of new infections and prevent the medical system from being overloaded. Several hot spots around the country exploded with new cases, some communities reporting hundreds per day. When the city of New York and surrounding areas were hit particularly hard, the government began to discuss an emergency plan to deal with emergency room overloading and the growing number of deaths.

One morning, news reported that the Federal Emergency Management Agency (FEMA) had sent eighty-five refrigerated trucks to New York City to assist the local morgue in storing the bodies of those who had died from COVID-19. As all this was going on in the United States, we stayed in close contact with our team in Israel to check on their families and how the community in Jerusalem was being affected. The challenges of life under quarantine reach far beyond the threat of the virus. Everyone reacts differently to isolation, and different personalities must find different ways to cope with the new reality.

Israel canceled almost all air travel and mandated quarantine to within one hundred meters of the home. Many of our friends found themselves jogging back and forth from the front door for exercise. Families with small children had it even harder as boredom set in and parents had to look for increasingly creative ways to entertain the whole family. Explaining what was going on to children also presented a challenge, as no one in the last couple of generations had experienced anything such as this.

While families were learning to cope with the new reality at home, the news continued to report the ever-increasing caseload. At first it was by the hundreds and then by the thousands. At some point along the way I lost count and started to realize the toll that checking the news several times a day had been taking on me. Feeling beat-up and worn, I cried out to the Lord for my strength to be renewed, and that I would see beyond the physical effects of this warfare and into the spiritual root.

Not long after, Amber and I had a remote video meeting with our staff from Israel. It was good to catch up with everyone and hear how things were going in Jerusalem. Before the meeting ended, one of our staff members told us that the day before, he had taken his son to the north of Israel to join his military unit on base. Before returning to Jerusalem, he felt the Lord had prompted him to drive farther north to pray at a place called Caesarea Philippi. In the Hellenistic period this same location was named Panias by the Greeks in reference to their god Pan. Today you can still visit the ruins of this temple, which was built around the streams of Banias in the Golan Heights. Prominently featured at this site is a cave where sacrifices were made and many detestable acts performed in honor of the spirit of Pan. Ancient pagans believed that this cave itself was the gate of hell.

As I heard this, God reminded me of another encounter I had with the spirit of Pan several years before. (Please refer to chapter 3 for a reminder of this story.) I was also surprised to learn that the Israel museum had just ended an exhibition on Pan in January around the same time COVID-19 began to spread internationally. Then the Lord showed me a picture of how those things that are released in the spiritual realm manifest physically.

Pan is known as the God of nature in Greek mythology, and the word *panic* refers to the frenzy that his followers go into when he plays his flute. The word *pandemic* also comes from Greek, and it means all people. As I began to ponder all this information, I saw how this pandemic had been released from the gates of hell to cause panic. A virus that jumps from nature into the human population and causes a pandemic is such a clear picture of how demonic spirits operate to cause fear, terror, and panic when the gates of hell are opened and they are allowed to roam freely.

When Jesus and His disciples once arrived in Caesarea Philippi, Jesus asked them who they thought He was. Peter answered that Jesus was the Messiah. Then Jesus spoke to Peter and said:

> And I tell you that you are Peter, and on this rock I will build my church, and the gates of Hades will not overcome it. I will give you the keys of the kingdom of heaven; whatever you bind on earth will be bound in heaven, and whatever you loose on earth will be loosed in heaven.
> —MATTHEW 16:18–19

How remarkable is it that Jesus took His disciples to this very place to teach them about loosing and binding spirits, saying that the keys of the kingdom of heaven would be given to His church and the gates of hell would not prevail! As God reveals who the enemy is, He will uncover a strategy of intercession to bind and loose powers and principalities of the air.

Chapter 8

MOVING THROUGH TRAUMA TO **JOY** AND **WHOLENESS**

As long as I (Daniel) have known Amber, she has made the statement, "Life can be very hard!" I agree with her, but my life and testimony were very different from hers. Growing up in my home, we had some sibling rivalry, and my parents had arguments from time to time, but we had mostly normal stresses. As I matured and became an adult, I went to work in law enforcement and had to learn to deal with the warfare of being a police officer. Over the years that Amber and I have been married, I have grown to understand her testimony from an entirely different perspective.

Amber's story is one of overcoming layers of trauma. I've learned so much from the way she expresses herself. However, I did have to learn how her emotions had a voice. I've watched Amber mature in her walk with the Lord and overcome many key traumatic situations associated with her past. Our tests become God's testimonies, and hers sure have. God will often call on us to share our testimonies in order to complete the restoration. Following is Amber's key testimony.

AMBER PIERCE'S STORY

As a mother of three, I love my children dearly and do not want them to experience certain traumas that I did and have to recover. In my walk with the Lord, He has grown me and healed me of much.

My mother got pregnant out of wedlock and had a child at the age of fifteen. Her parents had a houseful of young children and could not care for another baby. Because of the situation, she gave her firstborn son up for adoption. She was sent away to have the baby in secret and struggled emotionally during the pregnancy because there was no one around to comfort her. After giving birth, she returned home and found herself pressured to keep the pregnancy a secret. At the age of nineteen my mother got pregnant out of wedlock again, and I was that baby.

She and my father decided to get married, which began to set the course for my future. Even their decision to marry was traumatic because my dad would not have been the choice in my mother's family. She came from a long line of doctors, engineers, geologists, and teachers who believed in the value of education. My dad was just a good ole working boy from south Louisiana. He was a likable guy but not well educated.

Once a womb has experienced trauma, that trauma dwells there for the next child unless the curse is broken. There was so much trauma surrounding my birth that wasn't broken. On one hand, my family was getting a grandchild. In my mom's mind, however, I was the child she got to keep when she still missed her first child tremendously. It seemed that in some sense she resented having me instead of her previous child.

When I was young, it always felt as if my mom was competing with me. We would play cards, for example, and she would never let me win because she always had to. I remember many little things such as that growing up. Later in life I would come to realize that some of the things she did came from a spirit of jealousy. My mother also sowed division between my middle sister and me. I came to realize that the root of her jealousy toward me was linked to being forced to give up my half brother at birth.

Eventually my mother was diagnosed with bipolar disorder resulting in a split personality. Her original name was Barbara, but she took on the nickname of Babbie as a child, since her grandmother was also named Barbara. However, on different days of the week she would dress differently and go by different names. Her voice might change when other personalities would flare up, and she would insist on being called Baby or Babs (rather than Babbie) and would wear her hair in pigtails and dress in Daisy Duke shorts. Some days she would insist on being called by a different name, and even us kids needed to use Baby or Babs instead of calling her Mom.

My mother was also physically abusive. In explosions of anger she would pick up anything she could reach to beat me and my sisters. Many times we had bruises from hair brushes, shoes, brooms, and other readily available items she could throw or strike us with. One day she even chased me around the house with a knife! I normally had a friend with me who would see these very embarrassing moments, and on that specific day, I did indeed have a friend visiting. Needless to say, our home environment was not peaceful or a sanctuary that made anyone feel safe.

My dad worked hard but was on the road a lot. He was employed by my grandfather and served as a consultant in his car dealerships. My grandfather eventually grew to respect my dad and believed he was the only one who could run his businesses effectively.

THE OCCULT INFLUENCE IN MY LIFE

My mother developed many infirmities that manifested in various different ailments during her life. She visited psychics and other occult practitioners in her pursuit of clarity in her life. One time she took me and my younger sister into a voodoo shop in New Orleans to consult a psychic. My sister and I walked through the store looking at all the talismans and animal parts that were for sale. Even though it was before I began my walk with the Lord, I sensed the sinister heaviness of witchcraft in that atmosphere. While we were in the store, we saw glass jars that had animal parts and what looked like monkey brains preserved in a liquid. When we saw the brains, my sister, who was only eight, began screaming wildly and crying that she wanted to go home. My mother came into the room yelling and told us to be quiet. My sister and I were forced to wait in that horrendous place until she finished consulting with the psychic in a back room.

My mother continued consulting with psychics for years, which led to an obsession with the occult. All the while, her illness continued to worsen and the curses that manifested in her life only became stronger. I have always believed that her struggle with multiple sclerosis and split personalities was a result of an occult root operating in her life. This started with the trauma of not being able to keep her baby, and the secrecy of trying to hide her pregnancy. Keeping that secret was painful and ultimately led to her sickness, mental health issues, and violence. Her trauma became the ruling stronghold that the enemy would use to bring destruction into my family. Early in our marriage I shared with Daniel how I saw my mother's life deteriorating.

GARDEN CITY HOUSE

When thinking about the occult portion of my mother's life, I go back to when I was twelve. My grandfather had purchased an old, seven-thousand-square-foot home in Louisiana for my great-grandmother to live in. She spent one night in the house and vowed she would never return. As crazy as it sounds, the house remained empty for years. Eventually my parents decided to move back from Texas to Louisiana and live in that house. Many people from the area would not come to the house because of the stories of it being haunted. The reputation of a haunted house on the bayou evoked many frightful thoughts.

This plantation house was completely demonized, and our family experienced fear while living there. It seemed as if there was always someone watching me from behind. Doorknobs would turn by themselves, and things would move around. There were unusual sounds and even apparitions of people walking who were not alive. The story of the house was that the husband had locked his wife in the attic and starved her to death. We would never get near the attic! My dad hated that house.

After Daniel and I married, we drove past the house once and stopped. We knew the family living there had purchased the house from my grandfather a few years before. Upon meeting the owner, we found out she was a Spirit-filled believer who follows Glory of Zion and worked for the FBI. She showed us masonic and demonic symbols that had been uncovered upon her occupying the home. One of the family members even discussed that someone chased her through the house with a knife. This confirmed to me that all I just said was not my imagination, but I had been traumatized by spirits when living in that house.

Because of the fear of the occult, I was never drawn to participate in any of its practices, but I had no doubt that the supernatural was real. I tried to stay away from any forms of the dark side of the supernatural. One of my friends came up from Weatherford and noticed things in my dorm room at TWU that were occult— I had no clue. Then I got my future father-in-law's book *Ridding Your Home of Spiritual Darkness* and identified with so much of it. The book helped me tremendously.

GROWING UP WHERE SECRETS WERE PROTECTED

Wanting to have a good reputation is not a bad thing, but pursuing it will limit your freedom. When I grew up in Louisiana, witchcraft was part of the atmosphere. It was a way of life along the bayou. Some of my family had been involved in witchcraft, and it became one of the many layers I had to work through.

Today, with my own children, I can see clearly that there are so many occult things trying to get access to their lives. Parents have to seek the Lord on how to walk out their relationship in this world with their children. My goal is to teach our children never to believe a lie—no matter how small the lie is. Believing a lie can keep them from understanding who they are. Daniel and I are also teaching them about the dark side of the supernatural realm—that it is real but dangerous. Yet we also want to be careful not to reject the authentic supernatural that is from God while rejecting the counterfeit from the enemy. While we must be wise and use discernment, we don't have to be fearful.

THE TRAUMA OF MOVING

We moved back and forth between Louisiana and Texas throughout my childhood. I was about eight years old the first time my parents moved us to Texas. Later on, my dad shared with Daniel and me that he had moved the family to Texas to escape gambling debts. He had developed some dangerous relationships with people in Louisiana. Most of my life I believed that my dad had moved us to Texas because the economy had gotten bad in Louisiana, which I still believe is partially true.

We finally settled in Weatherford, Texas, when I was fourteen. Our move to Weatherford came with many challenges. Because my school and social life were rooted in Round Rock, Texas, it was incredibly difficult to pull up those roots and replant them in a new place. I had been the head cheerleader at my school and was socially involved with the Fellowship of Christian Athletes. After the move, I had to find a way to survive in the midst of all the chaos that surrounded my home. I had developed eating disorders and intense anxiety. My boyfriend soon became a survival mechanism. He would pick me up and take me to his house so his mom could help me process everything that was going on in my life. She was a strong believer and spoke the truth into my life at a time when I needed it most.

I hated going to school, but God blessed me with good friends, and eventually we became like a family. We all had problems in our lives, but we were one another's strength through hard times. I was never a good student, but going to school was a way to cope since I could be with friends. Each day when it was time to return home, I cringed knowing that the cycle of trauma was about to start all over again.

I excelled in social interaction—which I still do. God put favor on me and used that part of my personality as a gift to surround me with those He knew I needed in my life. By the time I got to college, though, I would have to deal with my biggest trauma—alcohol. Up to that point, I had not been exposed to drinking alcohol, but at the beginning of my senior year, at the age of eighteen, alcohol became a part of my life. From the first sip I became a rageful party machine. Because I was such a social person with so much energy, I could do my schoolwork, exercise, and still party until the wee hours of the morning. But when I was twenty-two, something more traumatic than anything in my life happened that would begin to change my direction. I was raped at Texas Tech.

Because I had opened myself to vulnerable situations, I chose to not tell anyone—not even my dad. I felt partially responsible because of the lifestyle I had chosen. Guilt and shame overwhelmed me.

THE CLOSENESS OF A FATHER RELATIONSHIP

After the trauma of the defilement in college, I left Texas Tech and went to work for my dad at his dealership in Louisiana. He and I spent most of our time drinking together at bars during this season of my life. I had become an adult, and Dad became my best friend.

One night, we stayed out late and he told me that he was in a relationship with another woman while still married to my mother. This crossed a parent/child line that was a violation of the relationship we were supposed to have. Even though I loved being with him, he had created a breach of faithfulness to our family.

Then I found out that the girl he was seeing was younger than me. She was also a manager at one of his car dealerships. This was devastating. But there was more. In addition to all that, I discovered my dad had been using my name to take out credit cards and purchase vehicles in my name. His debts and issues with money forced him to use family members' identities to better his financial situation.

SALVATION COMES!

After all of this trauma, you can see why I would go to bed crying and wake up crying. I was an emotional wreck. My friends didn't know what to do. One friend even told me that if something didn't happen to me, I would either kill someone driving or get killed. She had come to know the Lord; therefore, she started praying for me. Salvation from a delivering God came into my life. A whole new life began. However, the trauma remained.

My desires began to change. I would no longer go out drinking and partying. Instead I would read the Bible and Christian material. One of the first books I read was *Possessing Your Inheritance* by Chuck D. Pierce. Holy Spirit would lead me to certain books, including many from Joyce Meyer, since those were in Walmart, where I would shop. I was thankful for televangelism.

Daniel, on the other hand, had grown up in a family that walked in redemption. At first he had a hard time wrapping his mind around where I had come from. I shared with him that our family had lots of problems and had many dysfunctional issues. After Daniel proposed to me, I told my dad that Daniel's family wanted to come meet all my family. He was uncomfortable with the idea and struggled with our decision to get married over the coming months. However, over the years, he grew to love Daniel.

REDEVELOPING A FATHER'S RELATIONSHIP

There was always something very special about the relationship I had with my dad. I loved him, even though he failed me on many occasions. As a child I always trusted him and believed that his intentions were never to hurt me. I found out later in life that he had become desperate in his finances. I watched him choose to operate out of desperation instead of faith.

Ultimately, like I mentioned earlier, he used my identity to secure loans and commit other financial fraud. After I was married, we got a phone call one day from a bank looking for my husband, Daniel. The bank had questions about a loan that Daniel had no idea was in existence. That incident resulted in a long conversation between my husband and my dad. Daniel's confrontation with him over that situation and on my behalf finally closed the door of being used for my dad's financial gain. My relationship with my dad improved in the next few years. God had to expose that secret root to cut a curse of poverty off from my family.

Over the years I came to understand how a relationship with your earthly father can affect how you walk with the Lord, who is your Father in heaven. Even though I loved my dad deeply, some of the things that happened caused brokenness. I had lost a tremendous amount of trust. This affected my relationship with the Lord. Later I had to deal with this loss of trust in my marriage, as well as trust issues with my father-in-law.

I realized I would still have to deal with many traumas from my family bloodline. The thing about deliverance is that you always hope you will get delivered in that one session or one week—if I could only be scheduled with a deliverance session, it would be the last one, and everything would be done. However, for me, deliverance has been a process that has gone on for fifteen years.

SEVERAL KEY DELIVERANCES

At Texas Woman's University I began to serve the Lord through Youth for Christ and finding key churches to visit. I did realize I was changing social communities. However, God took my social gift and used it for His purposes—from the party scene to evangelism. Perhaps I need to write another book to relate how my walk in the world caused me to become a witness.

Spiritually my family was Catholic. My grandmother had gotten saved out of the Catholic Church. Though my grandparents on my mother's side had Jewish roots and even some records, they too had embraced the Catholic religion in their lives. I didn't grow up Jewish, and neither did my grandparents, but my grandfather explained it to me when I was twenty-five. One of my sisters found paperwork to support this. Some of my family members recognized their Jewish roots. Gross, a Jewish name, was my mother's maiden name.

I didn't want to live in trauma, but one cannot make the trauma of his or her past go away. Little by little I had to face every issue. The Word of God commands us to take the land little by little.

> And the Lord your God will drive out those nations before you little by little; you will be unable to destroy them at once, lest the beasts of the field become too numerous for you.
> —Deuteronomy 7:22, nkjv

This scripture has been the story of my life. The nations mentioned in this passage were the "ites" of the Promised Land: the Hittites, Girgashites, Amorites, Canaanites, Perizzites, Hivites, and Jebusites. (See Deuteronomy 7:1.) These seven nations, described as greater and mightier than the children of Israel, were occupying the land that God had promised to give to His people.

I had personal "ites" in my life—traumatic issues. So do all of us. They just manifest differently. God told the Israelites that He would drive them out, but it wasn't going to happen all at once. It would be a process. God certainly can deliver us instantly and miraculously. He did it many times with the Israelites. Remember when He parted the Red Sea to get them away? Couldn't God simply cause them to take the Promised Land in a similar miraculous event? Sometimes God's work in our lives is instantaneous, but more often than not it follows a process, and that process is for our own good. The process can be best seen by looking back on progress over time. This is because God doesn't just want to deliver us; He wants to heal us so that we can be conduits of healing for others. God is ultimately about restoration.

THE HOPE OF FAMILY RESTORATION

After I got saved, I started sharing with my family. I had a heart to see all my family redeemed. This produced some hardship on Daniel and me as a young married couple. However, God put the desire for our family to become whole deep within me.

In addition to other family issues, we had to face all the issues of Daniel being a policeman. Personally I didn't like the culture of law enforcement. This created high anxiety within me. I had faith for him while he worked but also had nagging anxiety because of the occupation of the police force and what the other officers were doing. I trusted my husband but knew the divorce rate for police officers was one of the highest because of the stress. Most marriages don't survive. I had anxiety because one of my deepest desires was to see my family unit established. What I had gone through was the trauma of a family unit disintegrating.

God had to deal with my desire for redemption while still knowing our family had lots of issues. Restoration doesn't mean that everything will come back exactly as it was when it fell apart. This is so key for people to understand. I came to the conclusion that the trauma I had gone through with my dad and my rape at Texas Tech created a great mistrust of my husband. Of course this was baseless, since we had such a good relationship. Daniel has been a faithful, loving husband, but trauma creates a deep wound that impacts those around us. I have spent sixteen years of marriage redeveloping trust with relationships—both male and female—in our lives.

THE WARFARE OF ISRAEL

Daniel and I both knew that the Lord was dealing with us to submit to our call for the future. He chose Israel. My Jewish roots and Daniel's influence from a devoted ministry to Israel caused us to know that His will for us was Israel, the nation, and the Jewish people.

We moved to Israel in 2011. When we went there, my family

was still intact and I still had the majority of my blood relatives. Where I come from, south Louisiana, we are taught that "blood is thicker than water" and your family is your blood. In this ministry, however, we have a different concept of family. It's been so hard for me to learn this. God's Word says that when some of the disciples were looking for Yeshua, He said, "For whoever does the will of God is My brother and My sister and My mother" (Mark 3:35, nkjv). This has been a hard concept for me to grasp, and I'd say it's taken ten years.

The warfare of Israel became a trauma. Israel is an awesome place. This is God's land and people. However, you are constantly having to process religious groups and all the relationships there. I had to do that while reconciling relationships from my past. This produced another trauma in Israel four months later. The pressure of dealing with the emotion of Israel along with the emotion of my past became such an ordeal. It was all intertwined.

Israel went through two wars while I was living my own war. Still grieving my mother's death, I became extremely vulnerable. I had no idea how much trauma I carried from my childhood from that relationship, and I went through a traumatic two years dealing with that. I almost gave up on life itself. But I knew joy was coming in the morning—one morning—I just wasn't sure when or how!

THE LOSS OF MY MOTHER

My mother died first. I have explained to you the occult power in my mother's life. I returned from Israel and went to Houston to be with her in her last days.

Daniel and I started ministering from Israel to the nations. While ministering in South Africa, Chuck saw a familiar spirit following me and attempting to inhabit my body. After attending a large meeting, he called our room and told me. He warned me to be aware of familiar spirits because after one person dies, these spirits attempt to inhabit someone else in that bloodline to keep the generations bound.

After my mom's death, the familiar spirit tried to visit me in our home. God opened my eyes one night and allowed me to see the spirit that had haunted and terrorized my mother for years. When I saw this spirit, I couldn't move. Every time I would turn over in my bed, an image of my mother was lying between me and Daniel. Finally, after five hours, I asked Daniel to pray. He took authority over that spirit. I had made headway, but I knew that closure from the past had not come completely.

MY DAD DIES PREMATURELY

Recently my process of deliverance escalated. Eventually my dad came to know the Lord, which brought me some healing. My father got saved after we moved to Israel. His life changed for five years, but later he fell back into old patterns since he had not reconciled his past. This happens when we don't deal with the layers of trauma in our lives. My mother had accepted the Lord Jesus Christ as her Savior five days before she died.

My dad died a premature death at sixty. This catapulted me into reliving a lot of family history. Over the last six years, my family had disintegrated. I had no relationship with my sisters. I presumed my sisters and I would reconcile when my dad passed away.

We returned from Israel for the funeral in the midst of a significant, world-shifting pandemic: COVID-19. Things immediately began shutting down the week of my dad's death. We couldn't return to Israel, so I knew the Lord had ordained this time for further deliverance and restoration. Every time I go through deliverance, a layer of a curse is removed. When you remove the effects of a curse, joy is produced. The Lord renews our joy every time we go through a process of deliverance. This is the same as pulling a layer of a hidden blanket that keeps us wrapped in an old identity.

After my dad died, I was determined to bring closure to our broken family. He and my mother had divorced, but neither had remarried. I took the ashes of both my mom and my dad, who were not reconciled, and buried them together under a bench in the Israel Prayer Garden. That was a place of closure, since the Lord had used me to bring His will back into the order He created. The enemy had separated and created strife, dissonance, and confusion. But no, the will of God was realigned in earth as it was in heaven.

This was not the way I planned to see my parents' reconciliation occur, but God had chosen this route. Now I see them together in the great cloud of witnesses in heaven's balcony.

A SISTER'S WEDDING

There is also a generational curse of finding someone to reject. If you can find someone else to reject, you can seem to be repairing family problems. For example, if my mom was gone, then everything would be OK. Her death did not fix the problems in my family. Rejection creates the strategy of hell in the earth. Rejection is one of Satan's biggest tools.

While here in Texas, a family member announced her wedding. But to my surprise she excluded me from the entire process—including attending. Most of the family was not invited to the wedding either. When I was told of this situation, I felt my body going in many different directions. What I had hoped for seemed lost. The hurt and trauma returned. This brought up much of the isolation and brokenness that I had to deal with through the years. I was distraught and knew I had to come to some sort of reconciliation. Without getting my heart right before the Lord, I would lose vision. The future of my family would not be the way I had hoped it to be. Therefore, I knew there was deep trauma I needed to deal with.

After the wedding I knew I needed to close the wound of rejection. I didn't fully understand why they had rejected me until a member of my family shared a supposed situation that had occurred years ago. The situation had never happened, but nonetheless the lie had festered over the years. Based on this lie, these relatives had decided to totally isolate me and put a barricade between us.

I don't know how God will break this lie out of my family. However, knowing that the truth eventually sets you free, I did tell the truth to some extended family members. Past deliverances had produced a maturity that enabled me to deal with this.

A GLORIOUS TESTIMONY

Each year, Israel observes what is called the time of Dire Straits. So much trauma invaded Israel because of the people's fear and unbelief of entering the Promised Land. This resulted in their wandering the wilderness for forty years. Each year this created a traumatic history in the life of Israel. This year I had my own Dire Straits. Yes, my emotions were up and down and all around. At times I felt like I was a yo-yo in the hand of the enemy. However, God spoke to me, and something happened.

I believe the Lord revealed to me that your family is made up of those you would war with. I had to realize that Daniel and I had a call to uproot our family and serve the nations from Israel, and the majority of our family members didn't understand or support our call. Some of my family thought our going was unsafe. Others just didn't understand what we were doing. There were some on the Pierce side of the family that maybe didn't have the same call, but they could understand and support us as we went to another land. They celebrated the call we had.

As you have read, the last several years have been very difficult, with many family and personal issues. As I wrote, my childhood was very difficult because my mother was unable to care for us. This produced a lot of fractures in our family's foundation. With my mother's death four years ago and my father just recently dying, I've looked at these things and asked, "Where did my family go? How did I lose my whole family?"

Through all my trials Chuck and Pam have said, "We're your family. Can't you see that? God gave you a family." I've known that in my head, but it's taken me all this time to see that God does have a family unit that He puts each one of us in. He didn't just put me in their family because I married their son Daniel. Rather,

God put me in their family to support my future and call. I have brothers and sisters here in this ministry who understand that we're in the same battle. We have the same call together, the same purposes and goals. That's what makes us a family.

While I was struggling during this painful time, the Lord spoke to me and said, "I can take your pain and make it someone else's gain." I wanted to share this because I know I'm not the only one who goes through these massively painful family issues. I am not the only one who has been rejected by family members. I know that many of you have been hurt by family as you tried to maneuver in the kingdom of God.

We all want restoration. We want our family units restored. Unfortunately that's not what the Bible says will happen. When I first got to Israel, a friend sent me a scripture at a time when I was grieving over the past. Going to Israel was much harder than we thought it would be. She sent me Matthew 19:29: "And everyone who has left houses or brothers or sisters or father or mother or wife or children or lands, for My name's sake, shall receive a hundredfold, and inherit eternal life" (NKJV).

Some of you may not be leaving your country. However, when you do the will of your Father, you will be blessed and inherit a hundredfold and eternal life. I want to encourage you that if you have pain—pain over family matters, family rejection—your pain is Jesus' problem. You can roll all your cares on Him. The Bible says He endured the pain of the cross for the joy that was set before Him. And that verse is always in the forefront of my mind. His joy is our eternity, our healing, our salvation, our freedom. It's all those things. That's His joy.

A DIVINE RETURN

Recently I had a reunion with four of my high school friends. I kept thinking, "What will I share with these friends?" Then I thought, "These friends never gave up on me. Daniel and his family have always supported me. I am changed." I knew I could share how the Lord had brought many changes in my life. Jesus endured the cross for the joy of seeing us redeemed and that we would eventually enjoy our life ahead.

There is a certain level of joy that we would never come to know if we did not experience loss. The deeper the sorrow, the bigger our capacity for joy seems to be. After experiencing loss, nothing seems the same. The Bible is full of references about mourning being turned to joy. Here are a few examples:

> For His anger is but for a moment, His favor is for life; weeping may endure for a night, but joy comes in the morning....You have turned for me my mourning into dancing; You have put off my sackcloth and clothed me with gladness.
>
> —PSALM 30:5, 11, NKJV

> ...as the days on which the Jews had rest from their enemies, as the month which was turned from sorrow to joy for them, and from mourning to a holiday; that they should make them days of feasting and joy, of sending presents to one another and gifts to the poor.
>
> —ESTHER 9:22, NKJV

> For I will turn their mourning to joy, will comfort them, and make them rejoice rather than sorrow.
>
> —JEREMIAH 31:13, NKJV

> ...to console those who mourn in Zion, to give them beauty for ashes, the oil of joy for mourning, the garment of praise for the spirit of heaviness.
>
> —ISAIAH 61:3, NKJV

John 16:16–23 is a beautiful passage in which Jesus prophesies His own death and resurrection. Verses 20–22 speak directly of the sorrow and joy that the disciples were about to experience.

> Most assuredly, I say to you that you will weep and lament, but the world will rejoice; and you will be sorrowful, but

your sorrow will be turned into joy. A woman, when she is in labor, has sorrow because her hour has come; but as soon as she has given birth to the child, she no longer remembers the anguish, for joy that a human being has been born into the world. Therefore you now have sorrow; but I will see you again and your heart will rejoice, and your joy no one will take from you.

—John 16:20–22, nkjv

I PROGRESS INTO THE FUTURE

Having come from such a disorderly life, I am a person who likes order. I like to clean my closet out four times a year. I find things that I have not used and either give or throw them away. I realized this is the way our lives should be. Don't leave skeletons in your closet. The devil loves a dirty closet. He loves when you try to wear your last season of trauma into the future. Secrets give him access and allow him to make you vulnerable.

Always place everything on the table so you can review your past and get ready to go into your future. This will keep you free. The truth sets you free. I think freedom is the opposite of fear. Get past your fears; on the other side of your fear is a great reward.

Chapter 9

JOY IS THE KEY TO VICTORY IN **WAR**

C OME ON, NOW. How can joy be the key to victory in life? That's a mighty tall statement. "You don't know my pain," some may say, "or what I've been through." You can't just be joyful when life hurts. It sounds too simple. The problem is that we tend to think of joy as the temporary result of something good happening and not a lasting source of strength. Joy—what is it, really?

In life all of us are met with tough and painful circumstances that we need to overcome. I (Amber) grew up with my fair share of them. My mother had her first child when she was fifteen and was forced to give the baby up for adoption. This was a trauma in her life that she was never able to overcome. She had been diagnosed with multiple sclerosis and bipolar disorder. They also suspected she had multiple personality disorder. Her difficulties became our difficulties.

As you can imagine, abuse and instability in our home was common. My mother left our family numerous times—once for four months. Even when she was with us, my sister and I would often be left home alone for ten hours or more a day while I was only eight and she was just four. Growing up this way caused me to think I didn't need to listen to any adult because it seemed as if I was raising myself.

One place I found comfort was hanging with my five girlfriends from school. They were my safe place. We were like a family unit. The problem was that I felt safe, but I really wasn't. Hanging with my girlfriends so much led to extreme partying and all-night drinking, which became my lifestyle for several years.

Both of my grandmothers were godly women who shared the responsibility of taking care of my sisters and me in the summers. Every summer for several years my parents would send us from our home in Texas to live with my grandmothers, who lived in Morgan City, Louisiana. My grandmothers became crucial people in my life. By the time I was twenty-one, I had not yet met the Lord, and one of my grandmothers decided we needed to have a talk.

"Amber," she said, "I know you've had a difficult life, and I'm very sorry for the way you had to grow up." What she told me next would impact me deeply and go through my head on a daily basis for the rest of my life. Grandmother continued, "It's time for you to decide what kind of person you will be. You are the only one who can determine your future, with the Lord's help. The time is coming when you will have to choose not to let your past define you. It's already a miracle that you are not a drug addict living on the streets somewhere and you are very capable." This conversation was the catalyst for my future. Though it would be another two years before I officially met the Lord, when I did, there was an overnight transformation! The Holy Spirit visited me at 3 a.m. on Thanksgiving Day of 2002.

Depression runs in my family and has been difficult to overcome. This problem did not magically go away when I got saved, though for several years I coped with it better. However, when Daniel and I moved to Israel in January of 2011, we would take on bigger and stronger obstacles. We both began to struggle with the battles of our minds in a very hard atmosphere. Israel has so much warfare, and it would be the training ground to prepare us for the rest of our lives.

After experiencing wars and rumors of wars, one war came that I didn't see coming that I almost didn't win. In 2016 my mother died unexpectedly at age fifty-seven. We did not have a good relationship, or one where I would even miss her, so the emotions I experienced were different from those following most deaths. This was very conflicting for me. I could not see how she had made a difference in her years on earth, and this caused me to see life in a dangerous way. I fell into a terrible, long depression during which I was unreachable. I had no concept or hope of a future. The enemy had convinced me that anyone on earth would make a better wife to Daniel and mother to Lily and Elijah than I would. I could no longer cope with life, and a demonic spirit from my mother had found a host: *me!*

Our family went through so much as a result of my long-lasting depression. Finally I started to detect the Holy Spirit's whispers letting me know that I was the only person on earth who could be a wife and mother to my family. I had to be intentional in order to dig my way out of this depression. It was a daily work from the moment I woke up until I went to sleep and sometimes all through the night. Yet it wasn't the clinical-type work you might expect. It was the work of pressing in to trust God for peace. I began to pray as anxiety would encroach upon me, "God, let peace be my boundaries." It was a work of entering His rest and grace. Hebrews 4:11 says, "Let us therefore be diligent to enter that rest" (NKJV). Diligent to enter rest? This sounds like an oxymoron, but it's not. Entering God's rest for us requires intentionality and diligence. The result is that He shows up with His presence. God is "a rewarder of those that diligently seek Him," Hebrews 11:6 (NKJV) tells us. What is that reward? Peace, rest, and His presence.

Just like Daniel, I have always considered Revelation 12:11 one of my favorite scriptures. It declares that the saints overcame the adversary by the blood of the Lamb and by the word of their testimony; and they loved not their lives unto the death. As God was rebuilding me, He was reteaching me what this scripture means.

Day after day I asked Him, "What causes us to fight for our lives? Where does this desire come from, and when we lose it, how do we get it back?" The answer God gave me is that we fight for our lives and our future because He is the author of our lives and the finisher of our faith.

I had been perishing because I had lost vision completely, but when I remembered the story of creation—that I was God's creation—He breathed new life into me. The verse below in Hebrews shows us how Jesus went through the hardest battle on the cross for us, yet He still had joy.

> Looking unto Jesus, the author and finisher of our faith, who for the joy that was set before Him endured the cross, despising the shame, and has sat down at the right hand of the throne of God.
>
> —HEBREWS 12:2, NKJV

God takes joy in our future, in the freedom that we find through a life lived for Him. He takes joy that we have access to eternity with Him. I was slowly finding joy in all the things that I did have. I began to see how wonderful my kids are, and everything they did gave me joy. I began to remember how much I loved spending time with Daniel and that I am so blessed to have a husband who enjoys being with me. I remembered how much I love to cook, and Daniel and I began spending more time in the kitchen cooking together. My invisible enemies were finally losing a battle of many generations, and I began to enjoy the small and big things in life and everything in between. God always wins when we submit our lives to Him.

Even when we have forgotten, God our Father hasn't. He is always there to cast vision into our lives and remind us who He made us to be. Each one of us has a calling and a purpose, and when we lose vision, we can always refer back to that last thing He showed us while we are waiting for Him to unfold the new to us.

WALKING IN THE SPIRIT OVERCOMES!

Sometimes the very person or thing that rejects you may be what catapults you into your future.

Just over six years ago our family sought to join a congregation so that our children could experience the discipline of being part of a church body. After we had lived in Jerusalem for about a year, some of our friends began inviting us to attend a specific congregation. One weekend we decided the time was right for a visit. Arriving early, we sat quietly in the back, near the translator, hoping to just blend in.

Much to our surprise, the pastor approached our family and asked if we were fluent Hebrew speakers. After finding out that we spoke only a little Hebrew, he said that surely we had come to the wrong congregation because we were Americans and not fluent in the language. We then explained that we had only attended Hebrew-speaking congregations since moving to Israel and were comfortable in worship and with the translator who was present. The pastor then reiterated just before the service began, "Are you sure you don't want to leave? I'm sure you are in the wrong place."

As a now aggravated mother, I thought, "There is no way I'm leaving! I planned my whole day around this—my children's naps, along with everything else that goes into visiting a new congregation." We stood our ground for that one service, and then out of respect for the pastor, we never went back to his congregation. At the time, we felt rejected and confused and wondered how any pastor could approach a newcomer this way.

We didn't tell anyone of our experience that day or why we made the decision not to return. Then we began to count the relationships around us and realized that God had already given us what we needed. As much as we had longed for a traditional congregational setting, God had already provided us with friends, mothers, and fathers in our faith. We realized that for a season our lives might look a little different from what we expected, but the Holy Spirit was guiding and knew what we needed. Our daughter had developed a strong prayer life, and I began to thank the Lord for the situation that our family was in.

After feeling hurt for about two years, it became evident that God had set me free and it was time to forgive. While talking to my husband one day, the Holy Spirit showed me how it was this situation that compelled us to host our first worship gathering in Jerusalem!

I feel compelled to write about this because all of us have suffered rejection, and more than likely, most of us have rejected someone. We sin when we walk in unforgiveness, and we sin if we reject others. So, most importantly, remember this as you run this race of time and faith.

> Therefore we also, since we are surrounded by so great a
> cloud of witnesses, let us lay aside every weight, and the sin
> which so easily ensnares us, and let us run with endurance
> the race that is set before us.
> —Hebrews 12:1, nkjv

To walk in unforgiveness, no matter the circumstance—whether you are facing family matters, church problems, abuse, unfaithfulness, or a whole list of other problems—will cause you to slow down in the race set before you. I don't want to slow down any longer. I write this to encourage you to forgive quickly so that you will run this race and make your Father in heaven proud as He watches over you.

Consider Hebrews 12:2 again, that Jesus endured the cross and put away the shame because He kept His eyes fixed on the Father and the coming joy. I encourage you as you walk through this week to meditate on all these scriptures. Pray that every root of bitterness will be pulled all the way up. Run the race set before you and remember that weeping may last for a night but joy comes in the morning.

As I began to heal, the Lord reminded me of our first three-day worship meeting in Jerusalem. We had put it together in just a few days' time with hardly any advertisement at all. In Jerusalem the body of believers is pretty small, and things spread best by word of mouth. This gathering happened in 2014, and the Spirit of God was moving powerfully. People were being touched, and every day more people would come. In Jerusalem a meeting of three hundred is considered quite large. On the last night, the prophetic was flowing and worship exploding. However, the meeting went long past the time that I had told my babysitter that I would be home. An announcement had just been made that Daniel would pray personally for everyone in the room, but I was trying to sneak out to get home to the kids. Daniel came over to me and said, "You can't leave right now. You have to help me pray for everyone."

"I'm just not feeling it," I replied. "I've got to get back to the kids."

Daniel said, "Just put your hand on each person's head and decree *joy in the war!*"

I did what Daniel asked of me, and the whole time I felt silly and tired. I was just going through the motions. That didn't hinder God, though. When He wants to move, He's going to move. The power of God hit me, and everyone that I gently touched began to supernaturally fall down. Every time I said the words "joy in the war," another person would fall over. Then, as I walked down the aisle, people were falling over without being touched. It was one of the most powerful experiences I've been a part of, and was the catalyst for our ministry in Jerusalem.

One month later we would find ourselves in a dreadful fifty-day war with Gaza. How profound that the Lord would go before us and give Daniel those words, "joy in the war." It released an anointing that would sustain many in Israel during such a tumultuous time.

DEVELOPING AN ETERNAL PERSPECTIVE

As we let God teach us how to run the race of time, He will put His finger on those things in our lives that hold us back or slow us down. Learning to look at life and our walk with the Lord from an eternal perspective is a necessary battle strategy. We must keep sight of the victory we have in the blood of the Lamb and the power of our testimony. When we do, He will secure our future.

God often speaks to me (Daniel) about the importance of timing and understanding how to seek His purpose in our time. While most have questioned how we can make a difference in this life, learning to look at time as a gift is the beginning of understanding how God uses it. This allows us to see the value and potential that God sees in our lives, and He begins to fill us with a purpose.

As I have pondered timing, God always reminds me of this passage in Ephesians chapter 5. This verse is one of my mother's favorites, and she would often quote it when talking about understanding the Lord's will in our time.

> Be very careful, then, how you live—not as unwise but as wise, making the most of every opportunity, because the days are evil. Therefore do not be foolish, but understand what the Lord's will is.
>
> —EPHESIANS 5:15–17

As God brings us to an understanding of His will, we begin to act in His wisdom, and this allows us to take advantage of every opportunity He places in our path! There is a time for everything, and a season for every activity under the heavens. Most of us are familiar with Ecclesiastes chapter 3, where Solomon speaks about an appointed time for everything, including birth, death, war, and peace.

> There is a time for everything, and a season for every activity under the heavens: a time to be born and a time to die, a time to plant and a time to uproot, a time to kill and a time to heal, a time to tear down and a time to build, a time to weep and a time to laugh, a time to mourn and a time to dance, a time to scatter stones and a time

to gather them, a time to embrace and a time to refrain
from embracing, a time to search and a time to give up, a
time to keep and a time to throw away, a time to tear and
a time to mend, a time to be silent and a time to speak, a
time to love and a time to hate, a time for war and a time
for peace.

—Ecclesiastes 3:1–8

Understanding that there are appointed times is key to how
God works in our lives. Sometimes from day to day we see that
things don't seem to be moving very quickly on our behalf, and
it can be easy to lose sight of the vision that God has given us for
our future.

In the first chapter of Ecclesiastes, Solomon talks about
how wisdom and knowledge are meaningless. Reading through
Ecclesiastes, it becomes clear that Solomon suffered from a bit of
depression in his effort to find purpose. Many of us have experienced depression and loss of vision at some point in our lives.
Throughout Ecclesiastes we can see that Solomon struggled to
understand how anything in this earth makes a difference in
eternity.

According to human wisdom and knowledge, we have been
appointed a time to die. Our time here on earth is short. While
human knowledge has led to advancements in education, science,
and medicine, it's important for us to remember that God's knowledge goes far beyond our own. When we reach the end of our lim-
ited human knowledge and act in faith, God can begin to impart a
supernatural understanding of His will, as it says in Ephesians 5.
All knowledge is a gift from God, just as time is.

What does it look like when we step into faith? How does God
reveal His will in our time? It is through the prophetic. God uses
the prophetic to call us into His will and show us His appointed
times. Above all we must understand that no prophecy of Scripture
came about by the prophet's own interpretation.

> For prophecy never had its origin in the human will, but
> prophets, though human, spoke from God as they were car-
> ried along by the Holy Spirit.
> —2 Peter 1:21

It is clear in the first five chapters of Isaiah that he had a strong prophetic gift but had not stepped into the fullness of his calling. The days in which Isaiah lived were evil, and God had to send someone who would speed the cause of righteousness. In chapter 6 God commissioned Isaiah to be that someone. Isaiah's heart was willing to accept the assignment.

> Then I heard the voice of the Lord saying, "Whom shall
> I send? And who will go for us?" And I said, "Here am I.
> Send me!"
> —Isaiah 6:8

Right before Isaiah accepted his call, however, he was all too aware of his personal and his people's sins, failures, and limitations as sinful humans. Like most of us, he felt too unqualified and dirty for such an important assignment. Compared to God's absolute holiness, Isaiah cries out:

> "Woe to me!" I cried. "I am ruined! For I am a man of
> unclean lips, and I live among a people of unclean lips, and
> my eyes have seen the King, the Lord Almighty."
> —Isaiah 6:5

Yet through His grace God made a way by purging Isaiah's unclean lips, dealing with his guilt and sin so that he could serve.

> Then one of the seraphim flew to me with a live coal in his
> hand, which he had taken with tongs from the altar. With it
> he touched my mouth and said, "See, this has touched your
> lips; your guilt is taken away and your sin atoned for."
> —Isaiah 6:6–7

God saw that Isaiah knew his gift and was willing to submit his time. He wants to do the same for us. All He asks of us is to be willing vessels and to listen for His timing. After cleansing Isaiah, the Lord gave him the assignment.

> He said, "Go and tell this people: 'Be ever hearing, but never understanding; be ever seeing, but never perceiving.' Make the heart of this people calloused; make their ears dull and close their eyes. Otherwise they might see with their eyes, hear with their ears, understand with their hearts, and turn and be healed."
>
> Then I [Isaiah] said, "For how long, Lord?" And he answered:
>
> "Until the cities lie ruined and without inhabitant, until the houses are left deserted and the fields ruined and ravaged, until the LORD has sent everyone far away and the land is utterly forsaken. And though a tenth remains in the land, it will again be laid waste.
>
> "But as the terebinth and oak leave stumps when they are cut down, so the holy seed will be the stump in the land."
>
> —ISAIAH 6:9–13

We can see in the above passage that as soon as Isaiah accepted the Lord's call, God started giving him divine instructions for how he was to act in faith. Isaiah inquires about how long he is to carry out these instructions, and God answers: until the cities lie ruined and the land is forsaken. At the end of chapter 6 God tells Isaiah that a holy seed will remain.

I love how Isaiah asks how long he is to carry out the Lord's instructions. I have often found in my own walk with the Lord that He will place a specific question on my heart. If we are asking the right questions, God will answer us at the right time. When we see things through the lens of eternity, the holy seed will always remain. God allowed Isaiah to see that his life had a purpose, even if he could not see what that purpose was. He will do the same for us.

We considered the lives of both Solomon and Isaiah to see the contrast in their mindsets. Isaiah's mindset was based in faith. He accepted that God's plan for his time here on earth might have an effect far beyond his years. Solomon was one of the wealthiest and most successful individuals in history, but he had already decided that everything in this life was meaningless.

BREAKTHROUGH

All of us face situations where we must seek the Lord's face for breakthrough. We must be dependent on God, as only He can take control of those places that have been bound up by the enemy. Intercession for breakthrough in this way often involves seasons of waiting on God as well as warring with the enemy. Personal experience has taught me that waiting can be the hardest part.

When I looked up *breakthrough* in the dictionary, I found this definition: "An offensive military assault that penetrates and carries beyond a defensive line. An act or instance of moving through or beyond an obstacle."[1] There are places in our lives that have been bound up for a time and half a time, but powers and principalities must come down for the Lord to complete His work in the earth. Daniel chapter 7 speaks prophetically about the beast and his reign in the earth. The beast is allowed to operate in the earth for a time and half a time, but when the time comes, the time is up!

While pondering this concept of time as it applies to breakthrough, I am reminded of the testimony concerning two demon-possessed men in Matthew chapter 8. In this passage Jesus crossed the sea and had just spoken to quiet the storm before this encounter.

> When he arrived at the other side in the region of the Gadarenes, two demon-possessed men coming from the tombs met him. They were so violent that no one could pass that way. "What do you want with us, Son of God?" they shouted. "Have you come here to torture us before the appointed time?" Some distance from them a large herd of pigs was feeding. The demons begged Jesus, "If you drive us

out, send us into the herd of pigs." He said to them, "Go!" So they came out and went into the pigs, and the whole herd rushed down the steep bank into the lake and died in the water.

—MATTHEW 8:28–32

What an incredible insight. The demons who possessed these two men had taken physical control of a territory in the earth and defended it so violently that no one could pass that way. When they encountered Jesus, they addressed Him as the Son of God and asked if He was going to act outside the appointed time. Even the demons know who the Son of God is and that there are appointed times in the earth! Again, in Daniel chapter 7, it says that the beast will attempt to change the law and set times. Reading through these passages, we come to an understanding that there is always a war in the heavens over set times. Yet the Son of God has control over time, and it does not matter how violently Satan tries to hold on to territory. Jesus wants to walk through those areas of our lives where we have been seeking God for a breakthrough. When the Son of God passes through, no power or principality of this earth will stand before Him, and we are set free!

I love the passage in Luke chapter 13 where Jesus is teaching in Jerusalem during the time of the feasts. The Pharisees approached Him with a threat against His life, but Jesus wasn't fazed one little bit.

At that time some Pharisees came to Jesus and said to him, "Leave this place and go somewhere else. Herod wants to kill you." He replied, "Go tell that fox, 'I will keep on driving out demons and healing people today and tomorrow, and on the third day I will reach my goal.' In any case, I must press on today and tomorrow and the next day—for surely no prophet can die outside Jerusalem!"

—LUKE 13:31–33

Herod was the ruler in Judea at the time, and a power and principality in the earth was holding ground in Jerusalem through the governmental and religious structures. This demonic structure was willing to use whatever threat of violence necessary in an attempt to prevent the Son of God from taking ground in Jerusalem and accomplishing His assignment!

Jesus was speaking directly to this demonic stronghold when He said, "Go tell that fox, 'I will keep on driving out demons and healing people today and tomorrow, and on the third day I will reach my goal." When God begins to cast out demons and to bring healing to the sick, He will not stop until His purposes are completed. John chapter 7 says that there was an attempt to arrest Jesus, but no one laid a hand on Him because His hour had not yet come. God holds the times and seasons in His hands. He is outside of time and controls time. Principalities and powers must submit to God's timing. Because it wasn't Jesus' time to be arrested, they "could not" touch Him. When God reveals His prophetic plan and timing to us, the enemy can't touch us either.

We can walk in faith that the Son of God will not allow any enemy to hold territory that is linked to His purposes. As we continue to intercede for breakthrough in every area of our lives, we must continue pressing into the Lord, and we must go on in the knowledge that He will not stop until His goals are met. If you need a breakthrough in your life where the enemy has held ground or some power or principality has blocked your advance, know that there is a set time for breakthrough. Wherever God has set His purpose, the time will come!

RELEASING REVELATION

When we break through, it often releases a new season of revelation. Amber and I have seen this at work in our ministry and as we have traveled in the nations. The Lord sets times for new revelation to become the driving force in our vision. One particular experience that we had was very powerful. We felt that the Lord was leading us to travel to Dubai in the summer of 2019. When we felt this calling, we did not know why the Lord was leading us to the Arabian Peninsula, but when we arrived, He began to speak in a profound way that would become one of the strongest prophetic experiences we've had in the nations. It is so important to see the hand of God in the earth to build our faith. Below is a letter we wrote while on that trip to Dubai. We hope it will be as great an encouragement to you as it was to us.

A PROPHETIC DECLARATION OVER THE MIDDLE EAST!
(JULY 19, 2019)

Amber and I are writing to you from Dubai in the United Arab Emirates. When I woke up on the third day of our stay here, my spirit came alive as God began speaking to me in intercession. *As I began to pray, it was like a window opened up to heaven and I could suddenly see the heart of God for the Emirati people and the people groups of the Arabian Peninsula.*

There is a new season coming of improved relationship with Israel among the nations, and as those relationships come into sync with the heart of God, a blessing will be decreed from the mouth of God over many lands and many waters! As the spirit of Persia arises, it will continue to cause the nations of this region to draw closer. There is a realignment taking place on the Arabian Peninsula and in the Arab nations that will bring many face to face with the God of Israel and the Lord of Hosts. I heard God speak to Yemen and say, "Peace be still!" and I heard Him speak to the Strait of Hormuz and say, "Peace be still!"

This morning, God told me to go down to the waters of the Persian Gulf and decree that He is a God who breaks the bow and bends the spear and tells the wars to cease. Then God showed me a crack in the foundations of Islam and told me to decree a shaking that would cause the crack to widen and the five pillars to crumble before His voice! *From here in the UAE, I decree that the voice of God will be heard like the sound of a rushing wind, and that His Spirit will usher in the truth of who God is.*

DUBAI: ARAB MEDIA CAPITAL FOR 2020

When I got up this morning, I looked at a copy of the *Gulf News* that had been left in our hotel room. On the front page was an article, "Why Dubai Has Been Chosen Arab Media Capital for 2020." After reading this article, I began to pray that Dubai's voice in the Arab nations would grow even stronger, and that God would use the voice of Dubai and the UAE to begin to unite the Arab world. I also prayed that this strengthening voice would be used like a trumpet in the Middle East to proclaim a powerful testimony in days to come. *Pray that God would ignite a burning fire of revival on the Arabian Peninsula and that a seed of revelation would begin to grow even now in this moment!* Additionally, Amber had a word concerning 20/20 vision coming into a new clarity, and I believe that 2020 will be a time when many nations see God defining their vision in ways that could not have been imagined.

A TIME FOR VISION TO BECOME CLEAR!

God had me read Habakkuk 2 this last week. In this passage, Habakkuk is crying out for God to restore justice. God tells him to write the vision and make it plain. You see, *God uses the clarity of vision to set a course for the restoration of justice for His people and in the nations.* We should expect that God will release clarity into our vision in 2020.

In this chapter, the Lord replied to Habakkuk's cry: "Write down the revelation and make it plain on tablets so that a herald may run with it. For the revelation awaits an appointed time; it speaks of the end and will not prove false. Though it linger, wait for it; it will certainly come and will not delay" (Hab. 2:2–3).

We must remember that God has appointed a time to release revelation and make it plain! Please pray that in every appointed time, God's people would be able to grab hold of His word and see the vision plainly as it has been written and decreed in heaven!

"Has not the Lord Almighty determined that the people's labor is only fuel for the fire, that the nations exhaust themselves for nothing? For the earth will be filled with the knowledge of the glory of the Lord as the waters cover the sea" (Hab. 2:13–14).

God's desire is to fill the earth with the knowledge of the glory of the Lord as the waters cover the sea. **Please stand with us in prayer that the Lord's glory would cover the earth, and that His revelation would become clear in the Arabian Peninsula. Join us in declaring that His Spirit will become known in all nations and to the ends of the earth!**

After writing this letter on our trip to Dubai in 2019, we watched in 2020 as Israel and the United Arab Emirates (UAE) announced normalization of diplomatic ties. This unprecedented shift will forge a broad new relationship and open the door for other Gulf Arab states to recognize Israel. Just as the Lord had spoken to me, the UAE came into an alignment with Israel and became a mouthpiece on the Arabian Peninsula for renewed relationship with Israel among the Arab nations.

Only God can show us His appointed times in the earth and set the boundaries of nations according to His will. We have been blessed in our call to minister in many different countries and watch the Lord speak words of revelation to change the course of alignment with His prophetic destiny in the earth.

Last year we traveled to Ethiopia, Kenya, and the United Arab Emirates and watched as God spoke prophetic words into each of those countries. Bahrain and several African nations have also begun to move toward renewed relationship with Israel.

> When the Most High gave the nations their inheritance,
> when he divided all mankind, he set up boundaries for
> the peoples according to the number of the sons of Israel.
> For the LORD's portion is his people, Jacob his allotted
> inheritance.
>
> —DEUTERONOMY 32:8–9

If we honor God's portion, He will continue to bring us to a place of revelation in the prophetic, and our vision will never run dry. We need to be willing to see the will of God at work as it builds our faith and allows us to move by the Spirit in the way we decree the word of God over our own lives and speak into all of those to whom He has called us. We need to continue to walk in the prophetic as it is part of our foundation of understanding God's vision and everything He wants to accomplish in our lives through our calling.

Remember that God can pass through any circumstance, any obstacle, and any challenge that the enemy might set up to prevent you from becoming everything He has spoken over you in His time.

Chapter 10

SECURING YOUR **FUTURE**

I F THERE IS one thing we have learned living in Israel for the last several years, it's that we need the joy of the Lord to sustain us in times of warfare. In whatever form warfare might take, whether it comes as a spiritual attack or physical combat, it's the joy that only God can bring that becomes our strength.

Living in a nation that is constantly at war, we have learned that physical warfare is a direct result of spiritual conflict spilling over into the earth. This might sound like an over-spiritualization to some, but I have seen this happen on many occasions. For those who have experienced physical combat, you know there is a sense of cause that accompanies warfare that is difficult to describe to someone who has never been there. Even soldiers and policemen who have never experienced this often lack a full understanding of the physical and emotional toll that warfare can take.

As we walk out our lives with the Lord, we will experience times of warfare on a spiritual level that will test our strength. Spiritual warfare can have many of the same effects as physical combat if we allow the trauma to take root. As I sought the Lord over the concept of warfare, He began showing me how joy is the key to overcoming trauma and maintaining the vision He has over our lives.

In John chapter 15 Jesus is speaking to His disciples concerning the relationship He desires and how we are to remain in Him and He will remain in us. In verse 11 Jesus goes on to tell the disciples that He has made these things known to them so that their joy may be complete.

> I have told you this so that my joy may be in you and that your joy may be complete.
>
> —JOHN 15:11

Based on this passage above, it is a fact, and always has been, that God desires for us to live lives full of joy. Actually, joy is a fruit of the Spirit.

> But the fruit of the Spirit is love, joy, peace, patience, kindness, goodness, faithfulness, gentleness, self-control; against such things there is no law.
>
> —GALATIANS 5:22–23, ESV

When we begin to understand that God is the One who fills us up with joy, then our desire will be to remain in Him and for Him to remain in us. Joy strengthens us and allows us to not only endure hardship but also to gain strength and maturity from our struggles. Yet joy only comes as we remain in intimate fellowship with Him. "In Your presence," wrote the psalmist, "is fullness of joy" (Ps. 16:11, AMP).

In the Book of James the twelve tribes are instructed to take joy, even in their trials, and to look at hardship as an opportunity as the testing of their faith produces perseverance.

> James, a servant of God and of the Lord Jesus Christ, to the twelve tribes scattered among the nations: Greetings. Consider it pure joy, my brothers and sisters, whenever you face trials of many kinds, because you know that the testing of your faith develops perseverance. Let perseverance finish its work so that you may be mature and complete, not lacking anything.
>
> —JAMES 1:1–4

Just as a soldier on the battlefield gains an understanding from his first experience in combat, there is a strengthening that comes through our own testing that produces perseverance. On a personal level we will all experience the draining effect of spiritual warfare. We live in a world full of enemies who will persecute anyone who submits his or her life to God's will in the earth.

In Proverbs chapter 10 we see a relationship between hope and joy. When we place our hope in Jesus, He fills us up with His joy.

> The hope of righteous people leads to joy, but the eager waiting of wicked people comes to nothing.
> —PROVERBS 10:28, GW

As I began to consider the role of righteousness in producing joy, God reminded me of one of my favorite verses in the Bible, found in Matthew chapter 5.

> Blessed are those who hunger and thirst for righteousness, for they will be filled.
> —MATTHEW 5:6

> Blessed are the pure in heart, for they will see God.
> —MATTHEW 5:8

When we hunger and thirst for righteousness, we come with an expectation that we will be filled. When God fills us up with His Holy Spirit, the fruit of the Spirit will manifest in our lives. Joy then takes hold and it changes our understanding of our circumstances, and the hope we have in Jesus becomes the focus of our future.

> I consider that our present sufferings are not worth comparing with the glory that will be revealed in us. The creation waits in eager expectation for the children of God to be revealed. For the creation was subjected to frustration, not by its own choice, but by the will of the one who subjected it, in hope that the creation itself will be liberated

from its bondage to decay and brought into the freedom and
glory of the children of God.

—ROMANS 8:18–21

The Romans chapter 8 scripture above speaks of this world's
bondage to decay and the glorious freedom that is the hope of lib-
eration we have in Jesus. If trauma is allowed to take root in our
lives, the decay and frustrations of this world will be the result.
This passage also says that our present sufferings are not worth
comparing with the glory that will be revealed in us.

When soldiers are trained in the military, a significant amount
of time and effort is dedicated to their ability to disassociate from
physical discomfort in order to function on the battlefield. This
process, which takes place in basic training, is necessary to build a
soldier's ability to focus on victory even in the midst of extremely
traumatic and often chaotic situations. If you speak to a soldier or
police officer who has experienced this firsthand, most will tell you
that fear passes and the training kicks in, allowing you to act deci-
sively in the moment. After the fight ends, there will be a time to
address trauma and assess victories gained.

When the enemy attacks us on a spiritual level and our situation begins to look hopeless, we must remember what the Lord's
will is for those who follow Him.

"For I know the plans I have for you," declares the LORD,
"plans to prosper you and not to harm you, plans to give you
a hope and a future. Then you will call on me and come and
pray to me, and I will listen to you. You will seek me and
find me when you seek me with all your heart."

—JEREMIAH 29:11–13

I love Jeremiah's letter to the Jewish exiles in Babylon. You can
hear the will of God become manifest in his words as he speaks
to the Jewish people at one of the hardest points in their history.
God's will is to give you a hope and a future!

We know that God's will is to give us a hope and a future, and if we hold on to that in times of trouble, we will not lose sight of our victory. Now let's look at how God sets us at peace even in the hardest circumstances this life can bring:

> Rejoice in the Lord always. I will say it again: Rejoice! Let your gentleness be evident to all. The Lord is near. Do not be anxious about anything, but in every situation, by prayer and petition, with thanksgiving, present your request to God. And the peace of God, which transcends all understanding, will guard your hearts and your minds in Christ Jesus.
>
> —PHILIPPIANS 4:4–7

There is a peace that comes from God and it transcends all understanding. When we rejoice before the Lord and give our battles to Him, our hearts and minds will be guarded in Christ Jesus. There is a peace that covers trauma and allows God to fill us up with joy.

As we walk through life, God will carry us from victory to victory, and this will strengthen our testimony. Through my experience in law enforcement I noticed there is something different about those who reach command positions. A good leader will have a different presence than your average soldier, characterized by a sense of peace and confidence in situations that would cause trauma in most. This demeanor is gained from years of experience in warfare and the knowledge that victory is attainable.

King David was a mighty warrior that dedicated his life to worship and wrote much about how the joy of the Lord sustained him.

> You will show me the path of life; in Your presence is fullness of joy; at Your right hand are pleasures forevermore.
>
> —PSALM 16:11, NKJV

We need to remain in God's presence to experience the fullness of His joy. When we come before the Lord in worship, He restores our vision and shows us the path of life. When we go forth rejoicing, He will meet us in our circumstances.

Isaiah spoke about joy and how we can have confidence that not a single word the Lord has spoken will return empty or void.

> So is my word that goes out from my mouth: it will not return to me empty, but will accomplish what I desire and achieve the purpose for which I sent it. You will go out in joy and be led forth in peace; the mountains and hills will burst into song before you, and all the trees of the field will clap their hands.
>
> —ISAIAH 55:11–12

Allow God to fill you with joy today, and take hold of the words He has spoken over your life. Understand that God's Word will not return void, and allow Him to strengthen you in your battles. Remember that victory is attainable and there is a peace that passes understanding. Let the trials of this life become your testimony, and take joy in the fact that trials produce perseverance. Remember that God's will for you is a hope and a future!

Next, Amber will share how God continued her testimony by using a root of trauma *during a time of war in her life.*

FINDING STRENGTH

In the summer of 2014 Israel experienced a fifty-day war. Even though God had shown me that we would enter this time of violence in the spring, I (Amber) was not emotionally prepared for what was to come.

One night during this war, I decided in my mind that we would have a nice, peaceful evening—you know, put the kids to bed, open a bottle of wine, and watch a funny movie. However, as soon as Daniel walked out of the house to buy a bottle of wine, the sirens sounded! I carried both Lily and Elijah down the five flights of stairs to the shelter. A minute later we began to hear screams from outside the building and inside our building. Instinctively I knew this attack was different, so I began to pray in my spirit. Then we heard the explosions. Lily asked if her daddy was still alive. Like any good mother, I responded "Yes," even though I wasn't convinced myself.

When there is an attack in Israel, we are advised to stay in the bomb shelter for ten minutes from the sound of the last explosion. But these explosions were so close, and because of all the screaming I wasn't sure whether the building next door had been hit or there were casualties and injuries. Out of fear I was convinced that Daniel had been hurt or worse.

During these attacks, cell phones are often intercepted for a few minutes, and we have to wait to check with our loved ones. Finally, after a few long-lasting minutes, Daniel was able to call. He was fine. He asked me to come outside and see the smoke billowing very low and directly over our home. Three rockets the size of telephone poles had been intercepted by the Iron Dome. Debris was everywhere.

In my mind, the attack hit way too close. I felt I couldn't commit to this war. This resulted in a huge argument between Daniel and me. Against his judgment, I tossed together some diapers, wipes, and formula, then I grabbed Lily and Elijah and jumped in the first taxi I saw. We rushed to the airport and caught the next plane heading out of Israel.

I reasoned that I was trying to protect my kids, but Daniel saw things differently. He knew that we would be fine if we stayed in Jerusalem. What I didn't realize was that years of suppressed trauma had built up inside me from the years we lived in Be'er Sheva. During that time, it was normal to have twenty rockets land close to our home. The explosions would shake everything in the house. I handled those attacks in Be'er Sheva quite well, but once we moved to Jerusalem, I decided that I was done with war. I made this decision even though God had shown me clearly in a dream that war would be awakened again in Jerusalem as soon as we moved there. After spending one week in Texas, I decided to go back to Jerusalem, solely out of my desire to be with Daniel.

I had stopped watching the news and convinced myself that Israel was in a cease-fire. As soon as I got on the plane with the children to return home to Daniel, a man informed me that Israel was in a full-blown war. Then the plane took off and there was no turning back. The children and I were flying back to Tel Aviv no matter what. Returning to Daniel was great. He showered us with love and gifts, and though we were under a haze of war, being together was all that mattered.

Daniel pressed through where I was weak and hosted our first worship meeting in Jerusalem. Because of the war there was nothing else going on in the country, and all of Israel was desperate to join together for prayer and worship. The people were hungry, and God's timing was perfect. The gathering was truly historic.

HOW STABLE IS YOUR WALK?

This experience taught me about the supernatural and the natural becoming the same. In my spirit I knew something had shifted. God had spoken prophetically to me and said I would have to learn to walk steadily even on shaky ground, even when everything was whipping around me and I felt I was coming undone. I believe this is a word for all of us. Over the past year I have pressed in to Him to find stability. I have realized that to be strengthened for the future, I must walk in the disciplined awareness of His presence. I have to visualize the hand of God coming down and touching the place in my heart that gets wound up. When I feel stirred, I just say, "Jesus, touch my heart." I am doing this all through the day, and God is ministering to me and making me strong for the future. I'm sharing this because I don't believe I am the only person going through this process. God is removing the things that would keep us from entering into our promises, and equipping us for what we will need in the future.

WATCHERS OF THE COVENANT

The Holy Spirit showed me the words *watchers of the covenant*. I realized this was a call being extended to our generation and that it would be a struggle for us to commit to and endure it. This sounds easier than it will be, because we romanticize it, but it's a call of forever—to watch over God's covenant with the land of Israel. When I visualize this, no matter where I am or what I am doing, I see the Temple Mount. This is important because God used Israel to display Himself to us. If He is the God of yesterday, today, and tomorrow, and if He never changes His mind about Israel, then He will never change His mind about us. The way that God has kept covenant with Israel assures me that He will be constant in my life as well.

This is a war over whose voice will be heard from Zion, but it's also a war over whose voice will be heard in our personal lives. Saying yes to this call will mean a life filled with blood, sweat, tears, and sorrow, but also one filled with hope and joy. Our hope is in Jesus, and we can find joy as we are anchored in Him! Anne Tate, one of the prophetic voices of Glory of Zion International, told me this would be the worst of times and the best of times. This is true for all of us. We can experience amazing joy and fulfillment in Jesus while the world seems to be coming undone around us.

KNOW YOUR TESTIMONY

Daniel and I learned a lot as we prepared to enter our sixth year living in Israel. Most often when God brings us through something hard, it marks us in a special way that is hard to forget. God recently showed me how important it is to take an account or make a record of our testimonies. We overcome by the blood of the Lamb and the word of our testimony.

Since the devil seeks to kill, steal, and destroy, we must remember our testimonies. What has God brought you through? You need to remember what He has brought you through so that with every challenge and every battle you face, your last testimony or remembrance of what God did for you is always on your mind. For example, the nation of Israel has an account of many testimonies.

Daniel and I have friends who have fought some of the major wars of the country, and they know the goodness of God over that nation. I have a friend in Israel who once confided in me that she wasn't sure why she got married or had chosen to live in Israel. I told her that the enemy was trying to steal her testimony so that he could steal her future. I also quoted my father-in-law by telling her that God is not bound by time and He could go back in time so her testimony could be restored to her family.

When we don't know our testimony or keep a record of what God has done for us, we open a door to the enemy, and our vision is at risk of being skewed or even destroyed. Through living in times of physical war, we have learned that testimony is key to victory. This applies to every aspect of our lives. You must keep record of your testimony so that you triumph over the enemy!

VICTORY IN JOY

That first worship meeting that we held in Jerusalem in the midst of a physical war marked a significant victory in our testimony. When God brings us into a heart of worship, He sets our spirits at peace so we can hear His voice clearly in our circumstances. Sometimes it feels like the hardest thing in the world to walk out our trials in joy, but we must remember that God is the One who restores our fortunes. As we develop an eternal perspective in God's kingdom, He pours out His joy in a way that is overwhelming.

> May the God of hope fill you with all joy and peace as you trust in him, so that you may overflow with hope by the power of the Holy Spirit.
> —ROMANS 15:13

We need the Holy Spirit to fill us up with joy, hope, and peace so that we can overcome!

> As for me, I will always have hope; I will praise you more and more. My mouth will tell of your righteous deeds, of your saving acts all day long—though I know not how to relate them all. I will come and proclaim your mighty acts, Sovereign Lord; I will proclaim your righteous deeds, yours alone. Since my youth, God, you have taught me, and to this day I declare your marvelous deeds. Even when I am old and gray, do not forsake me, my God, till I declare your power to the next generation, your mighty acts to all who are to come.
>
> Your righteousness, God, reaches to the heavens, you who have done great things. Who is like you, God? Though you have made me see troubles, many and bitter, you will restore my life again; from the depths of the earth you will again bring me up. You will increase my honor and comfort me once more.
>
> —Psalm 71:14–21

Afterword

JOY—GOD'S CURE FOR **TRAUMA!**

AS I SHARED in the foreword of this book, joy is the key to us having strength. Let me repeat what I said: the Lord has a purpose to move any desolation into a new level of abundance. This is the essence of spiritual life.

Jesus defined why He came in John 10:10: "I came that they may have and *enjoy* life, and have it in abundance [to the full, till it overflows]" (AMP, emphasis added). People seeking to understand their earthly purpose never realize that Jesus has already purposed them to "enjoy life." Jesus is the Door to a new dimension of abundance. His voice illuminates deep within our spirits with these words: "I came that you might *enjoy life.*"

A GOOD DOSE OF JOY!

Faith comes from hearing—hearing when the Spirit of God speaks to us. Faith's counterpart is presumption. Therefore, one must be sure he or she has heard the voice of God. If the Lord came back to the earth today, He would be looking for faith. Nothing is needed more in today's chaotic world than a good dose of joy! Not only do we need to be filled with joy, but we also need to carry joy!

Joy can be difficult to define. Joy is not a positive attitude or a pleasant emotion. Joy is linked with delight. Joy is both an emotion and a fruit. Many levels of joy are also described in the Bible, including gladness, contentment, and cheerfulness. The joy that the people of God should have is pure. This joy rises above circumstances and focuses on the character of God, who originates and emanates His emotion through us when we experience His will.

The joy experienced by a righteous child of God is produced by the Spirit of God, who is working all things together for our good. This joy causes us to see our future. This is what makes joy different from happiness and causes us to rise above sorrow and loss.

We go through so many adverse, trying times as we walk through this world that we need something to help remind us that the joy of the Lord is our strength. (See Nehemiah 8:10.) If the enemy can remove your joy, he can remove your strength. Strength means the ability to withstand our next attack. Therefore, maintaining strength is key to our Spirit-filled life.

The incredibly hard things that we go through will truly become some sort of blessing in the hand of the Lord and will produce a greater prophetic fulfillment in our lives. Yes, a sad, bad, unbearable time can become a joy-filled moment when we place that moment in the hand of God and give Him thanks for the moment. Time then takes a turn. The harsh memory of pain from the loss of expected joy can now be redeemed. That situation can become a transforming work of grace that can be seen in you for a lifetime.

Sorrow and joy are firmly linked. Perhaps it is because the deeper we experience sorrow, the more capacity we have for joy. I suppose it is similar to hunger. The hungrier we are, the more satisfying a good meal is to us. God knows this. Although we may only see the sorrow and tears of the night, He has planned a bright and beautiful morning full of joy. Pam and I are so aware of this principle that we chose to put John 16:22 on the headstone of our twin sons, knowing that one day our sorrow would turn to joy that no one could take from us.

GOD RESTORES JOY AND
PRODUCES STRENGTH

One reason God may have for bringing joy after a season of sorrow is to bring a new wind of strength to our spirits. Grieving robs us of strength. There is a weakness that comes from such an emotional and spiritual load. But God knows that joy brings a new vitality and strength, "for the joy of the LORD is your strength" (Neh. 8:10). Joy produces the kind of strength we need to move into our next season.

Like the disciples at the crucifixion of Jesus, we may go through intense, and even confusing, losses. But, like the disciples at His resurrection, great joy awaits us that no one will be able to take away.

"Restore to me the joy of Your salvation, and uphold me by Your generous Spirit" (Ps. 51:12, NKJV). Our enemy longs to rob us of our joy and get us out of the salvation process. That does not mean that he can steal our salvation by robbing our joy, but he can steer us away from the forgiveness, healing, prosperity, and restoration that are by-products of our salvation. Many times he uses the same strategy he used on King David: he causes us to sin. Nothing will rob us of the joy of the Lord as effectively as sin in our lives.

But these are days in which God is longing to restore joy to His people through deeper levels of repentance. In repairing the breaches that sin has caused, God is able to restore joy. Proverbs 17:22 says, "A merry heart does good, like medicine" (NKJV). Joy works like a medicine and brings healing to our bones. That is why Scripture says that the joy of the Lord is our strength. (See Nehemiah 8:10.) Joy brings the power to heal and maintain the health God has for us.

Even though David sinned and lost his joy, we see from Psalm 51 that he was able to ask the Lord to restore that joy to him. Through the blood of Christ we are positioned with even greater favor than King David had to ask the Lord to forgive our transgressions and restore the joy of our salvation.

My prayer is that you will be filled with restoration, victory, and healing! Become the joy carrier you were destined to be! Enter into a new dimension of joy until you break out of your shell!

WHAT IS TRAUMA?

Trauma is a deeply distressing or disturbing experience that produces shock to our whole bodily system. This can be from a physical or emotional event and can cause long-term neurosis, which produces wrong thought patterns and thinking. Once you have experienced trauma, you long to be free but every event you process comes from the thought patterns that have been created deep within your mental faculties. In *Time to Defeat the Devil*, I share more about moving from trauma to healing and success.

> After Jesus was crucified, His disciples were traumatized. The trauma caused them to lose sight of the prophetic words that He had given about His resurrection. You find this account when He is walking on the road to Emmaus, and the disciples walking with Him cannot see. Not until they commune are their eyes opened to see.
>
> Trauma imprints in your memory system. Trauma is processed deep into the tissues of your brain (processor) and affects your thoughts (heart). Trauma becomes the flashbulb that creates what you see and how you define the world around you. Traumas can produce *lock-ins* of fear, failure complexities, emotional distresses, and anxieties. These locked-in emotions can cause your organs to overwork (spleen, kidneys, and pancreas) and create adrenal failure. Every situation in your life can be *seen* through your unhealed and reconciled trauma. Trauma, when not processed correctly, will shape your world from the point of view of the hurtful situation and circumstance that you experienced.

Tell fear and failure to go! Confusion and an unsound mind are results of a spirit of fear. The enemy does not play the game of life fairly. Trauma, when used by our enemy, will create a failure mentality and a confused perspective producing dullness, deadness, lost hope, apathy, and blocked emotions. Leave trauma behind and remove the dam on your blocked emotions.

The enemy's goal is to vex your spirit. You are created in the image of God. You are a whole person. He longs to sanctify your spirit, soul, and body. Your innermost part is your spirit. Your spirit is your eternal part. Your spirit has three functions: communion, intuition, and testimony.

Your conscience is the window between your spirit and soul. The conscience must be kept clean so you can see. During trauma, the enemy takes advantage of you so that you question God's goodness. If he can make you say, "God is not good, and He has withheld His promise and best from me," you will lose your power to see. When you go through a difficult or devastating time, ask the Lord to intervene for a miracle to happen.[1]

ADDRESS YOUR ANXIETY

In Hebrews 12 we are exhorted to lay aside every weight. Anxiety is one weight that we must lay aside. Pam and I wrote a book called *The Rewards of Simplicity*, in which I shared about the problem of anxiety:

> Now, let me be the first to say that just because you address the problem of anxiety, that does not mean the problem is taken care of. However, by addressing the problem, getting the issue in the open and out of the hidden recesses of your emotions, you can then start the process of healing and becoming whole for your future. Your future certainly will be longer if you address this problem—hasty, anxious people use more adrenaline than others and eventually burn out more quickly.
>
> During my four-hour meeting with the Lord, I started

seeing my sin. I started calling my thoughts what they were—my own thoughts exalted above His—*sin*...Here are fifteen steps I have learned to take to break down anxiety. (Note that the first one is simply calling your sin for what it is, as I finally did.)

1. Be simple. Call your sin—*sin*.

2. Agree with the Word of God.

3. Allow the Word and the Spirit to work in you mightily to make you a child of God.

4. Forgive those who have hurt you in any way.

5. Break the power of isolation around you.

6. Become vulnerable.

7. Experience God's love.

8. Be willing to pray for others in order to see yourself healed.

9. Let go and lose control.

10. Give! Give! Give!

11. Submit quickly to His will even when you are confused by a circumstance.

12. Resist the enemy's voice that convinces you that you have failed. Rejoice evermore and align every situation of your life with God's perfect will.

13. Learn to listen to others so you can sense their emotional communication within their verbal communication.

14. Trust that God can send help and intervene in your life in time.

15. Be simple. Do what God tells you to do.[2]

IN TIMES OF CRISIS

In light of the crazy times we experienced in 2020, I wrote a book called *The Passover Prophecies* that helps us understand this Passover era and how God is realigning hearts and nations in this time of crisis. This is a decade of passing over and continuing to pass over into victory. However, as I share in *The Passover Prophecies*, a key tool the enemy uses to block our advance is stress and fear. "Look at our own nation during this crisis, for example. Many people are living in fear...a natural reaction to stress and crises. But we must stay watchful of fear—are we moving in the Spirit to handle our fear and surrendering it to God, or are we allowing the enemy to infect us with his virus?"[3]

ADRENAL FATIGUE

There is a wonderful book by James L. Wilson on the twenty-first-century stress syndrome called *Adrenal Fatigue*. He shares:

> Repeated stresses, no matter what their cause, make a person more prone to adrenal fatigue. The effects of stress are cumulative, even when the individual stressors are quite different....Adrenal fatigue, in all its mild and severe forms, is usually caused by some form of stress. Stress can by physical, emotional, psychological, environmental, infectious, or a combination of these. It is important to know that your adrenals respond to *every* kind of stress the same, whatever the source....
>
> Because of our generally stressful lifestyles, adrenal fatigue frequently develops gradually. When this happens, the *symptoms* (what we sense and feel in our body) usually precede the *signs* (visible changes, and laboratory or clinical

test findings). As the problems progress, these symptoms and signs accumulate to form a *syndrome*, which is a collection of signs and symptoms attributable to a known medical condition. Unfortunately medicine does not often recognize a condition until it has progressed to a full-blown syndrome. By that time you have probably already suffered considerable disruption to your life and well being. A syndrome may require much more extensive treatment to reverse than early symptoms.[4]

FRIGHT OR FLIGHT?

We are all familiar with the human body's response to a perceived threat or danger. The problem is that if we do not learn to embrace the stress of the day the way the Lord taught us, we fall into fear, run from our responsibilities, or fight unnecessary battles. In *The Rewards of Simplicity*, I expand on the role of stress in our lives.

Two types of behaviors are important to our stress responses. They are voluntary and involuntary. The voluntary nervous system is linked with the will. When we desire to do something, we must consciously make a decision about it. All through the day, we find ourselves making decisions. When I was growing up, my mother taught me to get up each day and make a list. The objective was to complete what was on the list before the day was out or by a certain appointed time each day. I had voluntarily surrendered to my mother's order for each day. I had a goal. However, when you live in a life situation where you are frequently interrupted by violence, arguing and trauma, as I was, accomplishing your list becomes difficult. Not only do you become frustrated, but eventually you become defeated. Eventually there is no real order to your day, and your mind and emotions become stressed by each thought about the things you need to accomplish.

On top of this, you live with the anxiety of wondering what kind of adverse situation will enter your day and reorder everything around you. Your voluntary system wishes to speak, but fear overwhelms the process. For example, you might need to remember an important fact, but you do not have time to collect your thoughts.

All the while, the involuntary, or autonomic, nervous system is working overtime in an attempt to keep up with all the stimuli you are trying to process. The autonomic system controls such physiological functions as breathing, heart rate, hormone secretion and the smooth muscle contractions of the intestines. With all this going on inside you, you can easily understand why an inability to properly handle stress can so negatively affect your health.

How we perceive an event produces the basis of all of our communication. Perception is how we use our senses—taste, sight, touch, smell and hearing. Perception of an event in time is usually thought of as a conscious decision on our part, which we based on the facts presented. However, unconscious elements from our emotions are also factored into our perceptions. Anger, disappointment and fear create a tension that accumulates within the spirit, soul and body. This tension can stem from residual past experiences where embedded stressors within us have remained dormant. Some of these dormant stimuli escape us and may go unnoticed until pressure is applied. They are not always obvious in us or to us, but over time, they have weakened our ability to cope.[5]

Dr. Archibald D. Hart, in *The Hidden Link Between Adrenalin and Stress*, writes, "The word stress means different things to different people. It is a multifaceted response that includes changes in perception, emotions, behavior and physical functioning. Some think of it only as tension, others as anxiety. Some think of it as good, others as bad. The truth is that we all need a certain amount of stress to keep us alive, although too much of it becomes harmful to us....When most of us use the term, stress, we usually are referring to this harmful aspect—overstress. This 'ebb and flow' effect is crucial to keep in mind if we never allow a calming after the storm, the storm becomes a hurricane....It is these more subtle threats that produce the greatest amount of stress damage. Things that worry us, prod us, scare or frighten us—when there is nothing we can do about them—can be the most destructive of all. Perhaps this is why Jesus (who had many good things to say about controlling stress) told us, 'Let not your heart be troubled, neither let it be afraid' (John 14:27)."[6]

STRESS: A BLESSING OR A CURSE?

We all experience stress. How we process stress is critical. As I share in *The Rewards of Simplicity*:

> For forward movement, one must face stress. To move forward in our lives, we must process stressors properly. That way, stress can turn into energy. How you apply pressure to an object creates movement and momentum. Stress can be very good if we manage the pressures around us. If we manage stress well, we tend to accelerate into our destined role in life. However, if stress manages us, we are filled with tension and anxiety. We must divert the negative side of stress and receive the power that advances us forward to solve the problems of each day.
>
> How do you handle stress? Are you seemingly "in control" or "out of control" in the situations you face? How you perceive yourself and react in a given decision-making situation determines your stress level. Your perception of the situation and of who you are, as well as your level of authority, determines your energy level. Self-confidence and staying in control produce energy. This leads to accomplishment, self-satisfaction and forward movement into the role for which God destined you.[7]

CHANGE MAKES US PRONE
TO STRESS

I am a mobilizer and love to connect with people and encourage them to connect with others. In 2019 alone I flew over 550,000 miles to help align the body of Christ from nation to nation. I have traveled for many years, and daily movement is a part of my life. In *The Rewards of Simplicity*, I share how day-to-day change can impact our lives.

> For a season, Pam followed me as I ventured out to find my place in the world. However, cool, calm, collected Pam now loves her home in Denton. I pack and repack, sometimes three times a week. When I ask her to go along with me, she sees the process as a little overwhelming. She helps me pack, but she prefers to tend the home, her church and my family (who live close to us). She gets involved in city activities, attends Master Gardener continuing education courses and stays very involved with our children and grandchildren.
>
> When she was a child, Pam moved constantly. Each move became a major upheaval that required living in a new home, changing schools, adjusting to new friends, locating a church home and learning a new culture. There came a time in our marriage when she wanted to settle down, begin to raise our family and establish roots. Because she experienced so many life changes as a child and young adult, the stress of constant life changes now could work against her joy. I believe Pam knows what true joy is, and she knows how to experience the best God has for her life by resisting some stressors that could damage the God-given wholeness that is hers.
>
> I, on the other hand, meet the changes that come with travel into new territory. Dr. Hart, though, alludes that "change demands adjustment, and adjustment causes adrenalin arousal. Our complex lives, with the many demands for change that confront us so frequently, can significantly increase our susceptibility to stress damage."[8] While seeing the world, meeting new people and experiencing

the anointing that advances God's Kingdom is exciting to me, all of the stress that goes with this sort of life, especially today, takes its toll. However, that does not mean I do not like the adrenaline rush that goes with stress. After a couple of weeks at home, I find myself looking for my next assignment.

Many people never identify their boundaries, nor do they learn how to choose to remain inside the bounds that protect their emotions so they can live in joy. Many people like the "rush of change," while all along the change is damaging their quality of life. Dr. Hart continues by saying, "I have known quite a few people who have died from heart attacks. And most of these people enjoyed up to the last minute the process that led to the destruction of their cardiovascular systems. Remember, adrenal arousal is seldom unpleasant; it invigorates and excites while it wears our systems down."[9]

That may be true of me. The call that is on my life causes me to carry the burden of God's heart for the nations of the earth, even if down deep I know my health might be better if I did not continually process so many changes.[10]

FEAR NOT!

In *Interpreting the Times*, I share the following about fear and developing faith for our future.

Throughout the Word of God, we find these two words: "Fear not." Fear is a powerful, unpleasant feeling associated with risk or danger. This emotion can be real or imagined. The emotion of fear is a defensive response to a stimulus that has entered the atmosphere around us. This emotion serves as a motivation to escape to a place of safety. Fear is a feeling of agitation and anxiety caused by the presence of danger. Fear can become a way of life if you anxiously anticipate all kinds of dangers that could overtake you. Fear that is integrated into your reasoning faculties can produce great confusion in your life. Second Timothy 1:7 says, "For God has not given us a spirit of fear, but of power and of love and of a sound mind."

Fear can torment an individual and make that person feel powerless, paralyzed, and alone. Fear comes in many shapes and forms. Fear causes an alertness to arise within your soul. This is a wonderful emotion if it is under the control of the Holy Spirit. If not, the spirit of fear begins to control you and vex your spirit man, with a resulting loss in power as well as demonic infiltration.

Fear has a progression that leads to a downward spiral. Once one fear begins, that fear connects with countless scenarios that lead you into captivity—producing a lack of joy and a loss of peace.

Here is an example. The fear of falling causes you constantly to be unsure of the steps you are taking. If you begin to fall, another fear, that of injury, comes upon you. The fear of abandonment is initiated because you are never sure anyone will be there to catch you. In your fear of injury, you develop anxiety over how you will be injured and who will take care of you. You then have a fear of the future, over how your supply and provision will come. Fear leads to despair and desolation, and eventually your faith is completely overcome and undone.

Fear can be one of the most addicting of all emotions because of the adrenaline rush and chemical flood that occurs in your body. However, in welcoming repeated adrenaline rushes, you grow unaware of the stress that this spirit produces on your organs. Eventually, fear can be like a drug that you must have in order to live and to cope with the changing society around you.

Fear is based on something that you think *may* happen in the future. When you create scenarios in your mind that do not come from hearing the voice of God, the grinding mental process that occurs within you causes a friction in your soul, which eventually results in many physical weaknesses and infirmities. Conversely, prophecy prepares you for the future, because the voice of God produces faith. *Fear is the opposite of love and negates the working of faith.* Fear is a projection of your mind and reasoning that brings you into enmity with the God who created you and sent His Son to redeem you, giving you eternal victory over death. The greatest of fears seems to be the fear of death. Hebrews 2:14–15 says that when your love is pure, all spirits of fear are bound from operating within your soul.

One of the greatest fears known to man is fear of the dark. When the time came for the Lord to liberate His people and press them out of bondage and into their promise, He sent a plague of darkness upon those holding them in bondage. In the plague of darkness, God demonstrated His power over the sun. The sun was Egypt's greatest symbol of worship. Pharaoh was considered the incarnation of the sun god Ra. Therefore, this plague showed that the one true God, Jehovah, had power over light and was Himself light! This demonstration of the Lord's power brought great confusion to the world system of that day. For those aligned with darkness, this brought great fear. However, those who trusted in God were secure.

LET FEAR WORK TO
YOUR ADVANTAGE

Fear can work with your intuition to help in the process of guarding and protecting your life and what belongs to you. When you get a *feeling of fear*, that can be a form of discernment allowing you to know that something isn't right in your environment. I believe that if you develop your prophetic and predictive skills in the Spirit, fear can turn into great insight. If you deny the emotion of fear, you can lose sight of danger around you. Similarly, if the emotion of fear is not brought under the power of the Spirit of God, a spirit of fear will take advantage of the emotion and control you so you fail in making sound decisions.

One benefit of fear is that the emotion you sense can predict what might be coming down your road. However, you must never fall to panic. Panic occurs when your imagination takes control of the sense you are perceiving in your emotions. When you receive a fear signal in your emotions, you must be careful to analyze what that signal links to.

When the concept of fear is studied and analyzed, you find that many surveys rank the fear of death and the fear of public speaking as number one and two respectively. In the fear of death, we are afraid that we will lose our last breath. And because many of us have never experienced a vision of eternity, we are really not sure what will happen after that last breath has been breathed. In the fear of public speaking, we are afraid that if we fail in what we are trying to communicate, people will not perceive the identity of who we really are.

You must learn to manage emotions that are emitted from the inward part of your being. Then you can prepare yourself for the future and even predict what will be coming in days ahead. Fear causes you to think on what might happen. Stop thinking about all the fictional scenarios that could happen, and instead respond by faith so that the powerful emotion of fear does not stop you dead in your tracks.

There are other benefits of fear. The reverential fear that there is Someone greater than us whom we can worship and adore leads to wisdom and action. When you receive warnings by the Holy Spirit, you become alert in dangerous situations. This causes you to even walk through minefields with confidence. As you rely upon the power of God and His revealed purpose in your life, you will receive grace to overcome any strategy of hell that has entered your atmosphere. To develop your true identity, you must overcome fear. (See Isaiah 41.) Your identity in the Lord gives you authority.

The Lord is sending a heavenly sword to you in the midst of the confusion of the world around you! This sword of His Word will give you confidence and equip you to *cut through* into the next stage of your life. As God's people, we need to be filled with new strength and joy. We need to learn to laugh at our enemies and the confusion around us. As we experience a sense of laughter, abounding joy, and the power of barrenness and drought being broken from our spheres of authority, we should wear a garment of praise for the principalities and powers to see. Begin to change your spiritual wardrobe to put on garments of confidence, strength, joy, and praise.

With these spiritual garments in place, you can have the same effect on the people around you as the spies Joshua sent to spy out Jericho had on the Canaanites, who fearfully awaited the Israelites' taking of the Promised Land. In Joshua 2, Rahab told the spies: "As soon as we heard these things [the testimony of the Red Sea crossing forty years earlier], our hearts melted; neither did there remain any more courage in anyone because of you" (v. 11).

We are dangerous creatures with great authority in the earth realm. When we are filled with God we should not fear, but we should proceed with confidence into the destiny that He planned for us before the foundation of the earth. This is a time in which we need to exercise boldness.

There is a great advantage that light has over darkness. The Holy Spirit is a witness to the light and gives revelation on breaking the power of darkness around us. Therefore you do not need to be afraid of the dark! Decree that any curse that has been spoken and set against you will be overturned. Declare that the bitter will become sweet. Shout, "My fear shall laugh!" Declare deliverance from any deep hidden grief. Ask the Lord for joy and laughter to arise in your emotions. Declare that your emotions will be healed and restored. Ask the Lord to increase your faith so fear is overcome. When God enters time and speaks to you, faith enters your environment and atmosphere, and fear must flee![11]

Let me give this final statement: No matter what we go through, God's love is deeper. Out of the fruit of His love, joy cometh!
—Dr. Chuck D. Pierce

About the Authors

DANIEL PIERCE was adopted at birth by his parents, Chuck and Pam Pierce, and grew up in Texas. Daniel and his wife, Amber, were married on December 18, 2004, and started their lives together. Daniel graduated from the University of North Texas Police Academy and worked in law enforcement for ten years, serving both the Denton County Sheriff's Office and Celina Police Department. During that time, Amber and Daniel had their firstborn, daughter Lily Pierce.

At the end of 2010 Daniel left law enforcement and went to work for Glory of Zion Ministries under his father, Chuck Pierce. Both Daniel and Amber are ordained ministers under Glory of Zion International and moved to Israel on behalf of the ministry in January 2011. Both have served the Lord faithfully in Israel for ten years and watched God give them two sons, Elijah and Charles. Daniel is the president and founder of Glory of Zion Jerusalem, a nonprofit organization, and manages a ministry center in Israel. Daniel and Amber have been blessed to travel abroad extensively and serve the Lord in many other capacities in the nations.

AMBER PIERCE was born in Louisiana and grew up between Louisiana and Texas. She was involved in youth camp ministry in her early college years. Later she was appointed the president of Youth for Christ and filled the office of evangelist for the Baptist Student Ministry on campus at Texas Woman's University. After meeting Daniel and getting married in 2004, Amber graduated college and founded a small business while continuing to serve the Lord through Glory of Zion Ministries. When God called Daniel out of law enforcement, both of them were ordained, and Amber moved to Israel with Daniel and her daughter, Lily.

Amber cofounded Glory of Zion Ministries in Jerusalem and continues to serve the ministry in many capacities. Amber is also the mother of three, Lily, Elijah, and Charles Pierce. Amber and Daniel have been blessed to travel abroad extensively and serve the Lord in the nations.

Notes

CHAPTER 1

1. Max Davis, *Desperate Dependence* (Colorado Springs, CO: David C. Cook, 2004).

CHAPTER 3

1. "Texas Penal Code Section 19.06: Applicability to Certain Conduct," FindLaw, accessed December 29, 2020, https://codes.findlaw.com/tx/penal-code/penal-sect-19-06.html.

CHAPTER 4

1. "Rocket Attacks on Israel From Gaza," Israel Defense Forces, accessed December 29, 2020, https://web.archive.org/web/20140804022213/http://www.idfblog.com/facts-figures/rocket-attacks-toward-israel/.
2. "The Charter of Allah: The Platform of the Islamic Resistance Movement (Hamas)," Information Division, Israel Foreign Ministry—Jerusalem, accessed December 29, 2020, https://fas.org/irp/world/para/docs/880818.htm.
3. Fares Akram and Isabel Kershner, "Violence Surges on Israeli-Gaza Border," *New York Times*, November 10, 2012, https://www.nytimes.com/2012/11/11/world/middleeast/israel-uses-tanks-and-machine-guns-to-fire-into-gaza-palestinians-say.html.
4. "Gaza Crisis: Tel Aviv Targeted by Missiles," BBC News, November 15, 2012, https://www.bbc.com/news/world-middle-east-20349280.

CHAPTER 7

1. Sarah Pruitt, "When Anthrax-Laced Letters Terrorized the Nation," History.com, October 4, 2018, https://www.history.com/news/anthrax-attacks-terrorism-letters.
2. "WHO Director-General's Opening Remarks at the Media Briefing on COVID-19—March 2020," World Health Organization, March 11, 2020, https://www.who.int/director-general/speeches/detail/who-director-general-s-opening-remarks-at-the-media-briefing-on-covid-19---11-march-2020.

CHAPTER 9

1. *Merriam-Webster*, s.v. "breakthrough," accessed December 28, 2020, https://www.merriam-webster.com/dictionary/breakthrough.

AFTERWORD

1. Chuck D. Pierce, *Time to Defeat the Devil* (Lake Mary, FL: Charisma House, 2011), 149.
2. Excerpt from *The Rewards of Simplicity* by Chuck Pierce and Pam Pierce, copyright © 2009. Used by permission of Chosen Books, a division of Baker Publishing Group. Excerpt is from pages 138–39.
3. Chuck D. Pierce, *The Passover Prophecies* (Lake Mary, FL: Charisma House, 2020), 102.
4. James L. Wilson, *Adrenal Fatigue* (Petaluma, CA: Smart Publications, 2001), 18, 11, 47.
5. Pierce and Pierce, *The Rewards of Simplicity*, 149–51.
6. Archibald D. Hart, *The Hidden Link Between Adrenalin and Stress* (Waco, TX: Word Books, 1986), 20, 24–25.
7. Pierce and Pierce, *The Rewards of Simplicity*, 155–56.
8. Hart, *The Hidden Link Between Adrenalin and Stress*, 50.

9. Hart, *The Hidden Link Between Adrenalin and Stress*, 51.
10. Pierce and Pierce, *The Rewards of Simplicity*, 170–71.
11. Chuck D. Pierce, *Interpreting the Times* (Lake Mary, FL: Charisma House, 2008), 35–39.